Walk with Me

Stories of Black Men's Resilience and Well-being through Twin Pandemics

Matthew L. Kane, PhD

Printed in the United States of America

First Printing, 2023

ISBN 979-8-218-26358-4

First Edition
Always Forward Publishing

Copy Editor: Jeremy Rehwaldt, PhD
Cover Design: Kelly Nielsen, Studio 92
Interior Formatting: Kelly Nielsen, Studio 92

About the Author

A therapist, scholar, researcher, educator, and advocate. Or, on the surface, a young Black man usually spotted with a slight smile and funky head nod that runs a tightrope to any beat between Kendrick Lamar and Isaac Hayes. Who am I? A child born to two parents, who, not without scars, climbed up from poverty and oppression in the unforgiving streets of Baltimore, Maryland. A man whose parents hoped for him the privilege of dreaming. Now a doctor… aspirationally chanting the words of Ms. Angelou, "I am the dream and the hope of the slave." But if you ask me who I am, I'll reply, as a practicing Zen Buddhist, with the truth: *Don't know.*

I don't know if I'm the perfect person to write this book, but I know I needed to write it. In the words of a mentor, this was a part of my healing process. And as such, I'm the perfect person to share it. While this book welcomes all, it is a compassionate letter from me, the Black boy raised around White people. A message to the structures, standards, and benefits of whiteness I was compared to, and simultaneously punished by. These words are a symbolic reminder of my unapologetic approach to challenging oppressive systems. My heart's intent is to find words for those with open ears to perceive world sound.

For me, building compassionate community necessitates challenging systems. In doing so, I continually aspire to a life that possesses the properties of water: taking any form to reach all places, it may be soft and refreshing or ferocious and unrelenting.

Endorsements

Winner of the American Psychological Association (APA) Society for the Psychological Study of Men and Masculinities Loren Frankel Research Award.

"Walk with Me" instantly draws you in with compelling stories, accessible research, and powerful lyrics. Matt Kane shines a light on Black men's resilience and well-being, two areas that are woefully underrepresented in the positive psychology and masculinities literature.

– Dr. Brian P. Cole, Associate Professor and Director of Training: Counseling Psychology PhD Program at University of Kansas; Founder Applied Masculinities Positive Psychology Lab

"Walk With Me" brilliantly centers the experiences of Black men unapologetically. Kane intentionally created a brave and healing space for Black men and himself to be and share their experiences with the traumatic realities of racism and whiteness during the COVID-19 pandemic and the strings of killings of Ahmaud Arbery, Breonna Taylor, and George Floyd. This book holds with care, gentleness, courage, vulnerability, and determination of Black men to survive and thrive in a world that fails to affirm the dignity of Black folx.

– Christiana Ibilola Awosan, PhD., LMFT:
Founder of Ibisanmi Relational Health;
Associate Professor and Director of
Iona University's Social Work & Marriage
and Family Therapy Program

Thank you

I know my words are limited, just as much as I know them necessary. To any and all people who supported me before and during this process, thank you.

For being spacious enough to welcome me. Thank you for being warm enough to inspire me, and thank you for being no less than who you are. This could not have become what it is without you… Mom, Dad, Syl, Will, Tevin, Kelly, Barbara, Jeremy, Hannah, Julia, Brian, Ngondi, Christiana, Donte, Jana, Aneesa, Sarah Jordan, and Lauren for your continual consultation.

I appreciate you all – Matt

Language

Partway through my editing I realized I made a mistake. Growing up, people in my culture, and especially those before me, often used words like *brother* and *sister* expansively. They were intended to reach beyond the boundary of blood and let others know they were family. I always relished this phraseology as I, a cisgender Black man, felt welcomed and included. When I started writing this, I wanted to provide that same feeling of warmth and inclusion. But, I erred. In a meeting discussing what felt like familiar dialogue about the potential harm of binary gender language, I noticed that I had not applied these lessons to this book. In short, I realized that not everyone may feel included by the terms *brother* and *sister*. So, I reflected and consulted and reflected some more. After this, I realized that I desired to continue a part of my culture, or more accurately my understanding of the culture, that needs to be expanded to do what it intends to: warmly welcome all.

I thought about changing the binary language of brothers and sisters throughout the entire book, but, frankly, that felt like hiding. I made the mistake. I would like to own both my imperfection and my desire to do better. So, instead, I intentionally left this language up until the point in my editing where I had this realization. From that point on, you will see me use the term *folx* to include all people, regardless of gender identity. Knowing there is no "right answer," I chose this path as I followed my own artistic vision of what it means to notice my mistakes and correct them. Please enjoy with care.

Table of Contents

Introduction

"Homo sum, humani nihil a me alienum puto."
I am human, I consider nothing human alien
to me.
Terence (Publius Terentius Afer)

A Comment on Perspective

I wrote this book to provide an opportunity to peer inside the experiences of Black men's resilience and well-being while surviving what I call the "twin pandemic": the global COVID-19 pandemic and a pandemic of social injustices aimed at them. If you're picking up this book, regardless of your identities, I appreciate your willingness to engage with this topic. Before we dive in, it's important to note a few things: First, it is beyond the scope of this book, and frankly any singular work, to describe the full impact of social injustices against Black men (or people with any subjugated or marginalized identity). Instead, this serves as my attempt to provide resonance for some and for others a small, but hopefully powerful enough light to encourage curiosity for you, the reader, and others to continue learning through reading, conversation, and living with a flexible mind that seeks to understand the deleterious effects of racism. Second, it is important to note that I, as a Black-identifying man, born and raised within the United States, have carefully tried to manage my own biases during the construction of this book. In a time where powerful individuals label facts as fiction and masquerade fiction as fact, I recognize the importance of thorough work. With this in mind, I did my best to provide diverse references for you as the reader, to consult with scholars and integrate contributions from various professionals, and also to address the multiple ways racism has impacted the psychological, sociological, and neurological lives of Black men, both directly and indirectly.

Lastly, I will not be coy in admitting that researching for this book was emotionally taxing; however, I believe that such research is necessary as we expand our understanding of the world and our role in it through a well-informed, contextual lens. I believe that there are no wrong feelings in this world. As such, I invite you to be mindful of your own emotions, thoughts, and reactions as you read, and push the conversation forward into your life. The words I selected were selected with intention. I ask that you do not rush to get through this book. Instead, take your time reading and absorbing the messages. During the year 2020, many individuals and systems made statements regarding the need to dismantle racist systems (American Psychological Association, 2021; Society for the Psychological Study of Men and Masculinities, 2019). It is important that these proclamations do not become performative and instead move toward well-informed and well-resourced action. To do that, I'm humbly asking you to walk with me . . .

The Future of America

When trying to comprehend the list of injustices experienced by Black Americans, we will quickly realize that they are innumerable. Moreover, it is impossible—and limiting—to rank the detrimental effects each, in their singularity, has had on the Black community. However, it is incumbent to understand the interrelated connection between the intentionally caused suffering of Black people and the United States as a whole. The discrimination facing majority Black communities is directly related to the health and future of America. This is stated much more poignantly by James Baldwin. Though he was discussing the future of America in an interview in 1963, his words remain relevant today:

> The future of the negro in this country is precisely as bright or as dark as the future of the country. It is entirely up to the American people and their representatives, whether or not they are going to face and deal with and embrace this stranger with whom they relied on so long. What white people have to do is figure out in their own hearts why it was necessary to have a nigger in the first place. Because I am not a nigger, I am a man. But if you think I'm a nigger, it means you need

> him . . . and you've got to find out why. (Baldwin, 2017)

While this book is not intended to answer this question, considering the contemporary climate of race in America requires understanding that historical and continued injustices toward the Black community are inescapably interwoven into the story of America and its healing. With this in mind, I intentionally placed the exploration of contemporary Black men's resilience and well-being within the abundance of historical racial events and interwoven systems of racial injustice. Today, as racism is challenged by some and given asylum by others, understanding the truths of racial injustice is perhaps even more imperative.

1

Social Unrest: A Legacy

Continued History of America: Social Injustice

With the oppressive heat of the sun long since fallen into a still night, I find myself stuck at this table trying to make sense of the mess in my head. The years 2020, 2021, 2022, as well as our time before and our time after, be it feeling or fact, I see clear the strings that connect the three worlds of past, present, and future. Candidly, however, I'm afraid I lack the ability to cleanly articulate the many stories to come in this book. Nevertheless, the discomfort I experience from my outward process has led me to a belief that permeates my fears: This is not meant to be clean. What we saw in these years feel like stories from the past: police brutality, over ten thousand demonstrations across the nation shouting for police reform (Chavez, 2020), literal and legislative battles over Confederate monuments, professional athletes standing up for social justice, racist political rhetoric and policy, a resurgence of overt White supremacy as a result of and backed by politicians and journalists, plus the highest recorded number of deaths by gun violence—with Black men ten times more likely to die from gun violence than White men (Wamser-Nanney, 2021). All this in the same year we would see our first global pandemic in over a century. And Black Americans were perhaps at the center of these events. For a while I asked myself where to begin; however, I have found that the most important thing is not *where* to begin, but simply to begin.

What is racism? Webster will tell you that racism is "prejudice, discrimination, or antagonism directed against a person or people on the basis of their membership in a particular racial or ethnic group, typically one that is a minority or marginalized" (Merriam-Webster, 2011). As I think about the ways racism was taught to me, it was often the case that it echoed this definition. Further, as I attended higher levels of learning, this definition was repeatedly disseminated to students and shared among professionals in academic and educational discourse. However, it has been my experience that this definition can be grossly misleading. This is not to suggest that the definition is in effect, *wrong*, rather to suggest that "racism" has a much more intricate, insidious existence within systems, between relationships, and within individuals, that without recourse, will continue to eat away at our minds and our bodies as it engages in its usual dance—with ever-changing outfits—down generational lines. And for awhile now, one of those outfits has been blue.

Black male Kansas Area Police Sergeant—

I felt pressed . . . Specifically with the civil unrest . . . there's a tendency I think that needs to be rooted out of law enforcement to not question some of the things that happen in law enforcement that really should be questioned. And I think George Floyd specifically was one of those instances where I would get some push back from other police officers like . . . "The situation wouldn't of happened if he had just complied. . . ." Whether it's the thin blue line, it is pervasive and it needs to be changed. . . . There's definitely a mentality that people in law enforcement have to protect each other. And sometimes that can be good, but I think for the most part whenever you get into a feeling that you're entitled to certain behaviors or you have to go out of your way to make sure the integrity of the thin blue line is maintained, that's problematic. . . . [And] in regard to your question about my feelings about minorities and the thin blue line, I do think it has been the organization over the community in some respects, and I don't think it's a good thing. . . . I think it's a police officer's responsibility to protect the community, it's not to protect the organization.

Policing and Black communities are no strangers to one another. With their differential relationship dating back to the inception of modern policing—which was designed to capture runaway slaves, and the Black Codes, which were enacted to restrict the freedoms of Black Americans (Abdelfatah, 2020), it's probably not a surprise that disparities in policing still exist today. Moreover, during this twin-pandemic they were expressed in a multitude of ways. The construction of race in America has been well documented through independent and federal research for decades (Dunbar & Jones 2021; Fredrickson, 2003). Additionally, we know that the social construction of race has done what it intended to do from the beginning—create privileges afforded to some (i.e., White people) at the expense of others—and many advantages remain embedded in our current structures. This was evident when people and systems enforced social distancing regulations during COVID-19. Data from the pandemic showed that Black people were at increased risk of police involvement, including arrests, when not following public health guidelines in comparison to their White peers (Southall, 2020). Statistically, Black people made up almost 70 percent of police summons in New York, despite only comprising 24 percent of the city's population. Similar rates were found in Ohio and in the city of Chicago (Evans & Bauer, 2020; Kaplan & Hardy, 2020).

One potential reason for this is the historical and continued criminalization of Black Americans, especially

Black men (Westcott, 2015; Alexander, 2010). Racist socialization serves as a catalyst for this archetype by creating implicit and often unconscious assumptions about crime and who—based on race—commits crimes (Degruy, 2017). This results in Black Americans, especially Black men, being viewed as more suspicious. When found guilty, they are also more likely to have longer sentences than their White male peers for committing the same crimes (Levinson & Young, 2009; Eberhardt et al., 2004; Spohn, 2017). Systemic inequalities extend from the individual level to the macro level of community. Majority Black communities have historically been subjected to higher surveillance by police. This, in conjunction with implicit bias, significantly increases the likelihood of Black men having to interact with police and simultaneously creates a protective barrier for White men and women (Smith et al., 2014).

Meanwhile, encounters with police continue to prove deadly for Black men. Edwards, Lee, and Esposito (2019) looked at data from Fatal Encounters, a journalist-led effort to compile a list of police killings. Researchers examined deaths by police through the variables of age, sex, and race. Findings were that Black men had the highest risk of any group for being killed by police in their lifetime, with use of force being among the leading causes of death for men of color. Moreover, death by police in the United States far surpassed the rate in other industrial countries. Consistent with this finding, researchers discovered that one in every thousand Black men in the United States is expected to be killed by police over the course of their life. These findings provide evidence that police violence needs to be treated as a public health issue.

> Daily the Negro is coming more and more to look upon law and justice, not as protecting safeguards, but as sources of humiliation and oppression. The laws are made by men who have little interest in him; they are executed by men who have absolutely no motive for treating the black people with courtesy or consideration; and, finally, the accused law-breaker is tried, not by his peers, but too often by men who would rather punish ten innocent Negroes than let one guilty one escape. (W. E. B. Du Bois)

In addition to implicit and explicit racism in law enforcement, the experience of dehumanization, defined as a denial of one's innate full humanity (Smith, 2011), can help explain the inequalities that produce crime in communities that have majority Black residents. The depiction of Black men as aggressive, violent, uncivilized, and inferior has been present since American slavery (Fishman, 2006). This depiction has been accompanied by a history of racial bias and violence that, despite mainstream platforms' best attempts to hide reality, could not be concealed. A short list of examples that overwhelmed their best efforts to hide the truth include "the war on drugs," Federal Emergency Management Agency (FEMA)'s response to Hurricane Katrina, mass incarceration, the case of Henrietta Lacks, the Tuskegee experiments, the beating of Rodney King, and, more recently, the killings of George Floyd, Breonna Taylor, and Ahmaud Arbery and the response to the COVID-19 pandemic. Criminologists need to include the historical context of racist archetyping in their understanding of the relationship of Black men with the criminal justice system. For far too long, this narrative of Black men as criminals has scapegoated Black men as a "problem" and justified racist propaganda. This in turn has allowed people to feel less racist about owning and vocalizing their racist beliefs. Contemporary examples include the "All Lives Matter" and "Blue Lives Matter" slogans developed in response to the Black Lives Matter movement; these messages directly defend our racist system while indirectly telling Black people they are the problem and need to fix themselves.

Over these past few years, the effects of social injustice within the United States have been shown to the world. It's always been a charged, divisive topic for many, and continues to be polarizing within the United States. One example of this polarization were the actions taken by the United States government toward BLM protests in the summer of 2020. These protests were sparked in large part from the murders of George Floyd and Breonna Taylor by police as a result of what many Black men have experienced as institutional racism within our policing system. Further, just a few months later and with increased polarization due to the political rhetoric of the 2020 Presidential Election, we saw firsthand stark differences in policing. For example, on January 6, 2021, large groups, including White supremacists, who did not accept the results of the presidential election attempted an insurrection (Chavez, 2021; Kane, 2021), despite sixty-one court challenges and multiple recounts in various states that found no evidence of widespread voter fraud (Balsamo, 2020; Cummings et al., 2021). While some were arrested on that day, those watching the events on TV, such as myself, could see many others walking down the steps of the Capitol, jovial, as they returned home. Despite large amounts of federal intelligence suggesting an attempted insurrection, police officials would later state that they were unprepared for such an assault. Further, some elected officials would soon try to justify the actions of the insurrectionists. Representative Andrew Clyde of Ohio, for example, compared the insurrection to a "normal tourist visit" (Sherman, 2021), overlooking the multiple deaths of insurrectionists and police officers, as well as the accompanying psychological trauma (Hermann & Thompson, 2021).

In contrast to the relatively limited police response to the insurrection, police responded forcefully to the hundreds of BLM protests that took place across the country to protest systemic racism expressed through police brutality, especially by the murders of George Floyd and Breonna Taylor by police violence (Beck, 2021). During these protests, former president Donald Trump asked for and received four thousand National Guard troops to, in his words, "protect" the Capitol from potential riots. However, public research found that approximately 94 percent of BLM protests held across the United States were peaceful (Kaur, 2020; Kishi, 2022). Further, the remaining 6 percent that were considered violent were not directly instigated by BLM protesters. Rather, much of that violence and looting resulted from continued escalating and aggressive governmental intervention, as well as instigation from right-wing groups or individuals, such as ramming protesters with cars. The criminalization of Blackness is even clearer when the BLM protests are compared to right-wing militias or social movements, whose actions were more than twice as violent than BLM protests (14 percent compared to 6 percent), yet those violent protests received minimal media coverage.

Tennessee area Black male Security Officer—

> T: Being in law enforcement for an African American male is very challenging. . . . [I]n regard to the BLM protests, when I was around white police officers you can tell that they were very uncomfortable. In regard to having conversations about BLM and about the deaths of innocent Black men. . . .

Matt: Did you feel safe being able to speak authentically, or did you ever get concerned about what might happen to you or your job security?

T: Yes! Yes! Yes! Especially in a climate such as the one we live in today in regard to the social injustices. You can speak on things, but as far as trying to voice your true opinions about how you feel and state facts, many people, especially in higher positions, they do not want to hear that.

Continued History of America: Redlining

My mom would often tell me stories about the neighborhood she grew up in—west Baltimore, Maryland. As with many people of her generation, she sometimes made comparisons between the decades. She typically used the catchphrase, "That's all you get," to let you know she was about to transition into a talk about the way things *used to be*. These stories often contained a sense of Black community where everyone looked out for each other—the phrase "it takes a village" echoes in my head. For many, this might illustrate peaceful pictures and thoughts of vicarious joys you might share with her and others in the "village." While many joyous events no doubt took place, what if I told you the "villagers" never wanted to be there? Or perhaps more accurately, they wanted the freedom to leave in peace. I often felt that the heart of these stories was not so much about how great the neighborhoods were as about how the community showed an adaptive resilience to survive their reality.

Sometimes I sit and reflect on just how much creative resilience was required of my mother as a young Black woman whose own mom was blocked from any employment outside the shipping yards, or a life lived anywhere that was not painted *red* and intentionally deprived of resources? This practice I'm alluding to, called redlining, originated out of the United States' homeownership programs after President Franklin Delano Roosevelt's New Deal. These programs provided government-insured mortgages to would-be homeowners (Jackson, 2021). However, our government added requirements to qualify for loans. In the process, the Home Owners' Loan Corporation, whose task was to make sure people did not default on loans (Gross, 2017), drew maps to show what areas were worth loans. They were drawn in colors. They were ranked. Green areas were "best," blue "still desirable," yellow "definitely declining," and red "hazardous." The areas labeled in red ink were where Black people lived. In fact, "the presence of negros" was one criterion for defining a neighborhood as red. In short, majority Black communities were called "risky investments" and residents of those communities were prevented from getting bank loans that would have allowed them to own their own homes and build wealth. I'm ashamed to say that it was not until writing this that I learned how the New Deal paved the way for this systemic discrimination. To add insult to injury, government policy also forbade selling homes in certain areas to "negros," which prevented Black people from moving to other neighborhoods. While redlining was made illegal after the passage of the Fair Housing Act in 1968, institutional racism remained entrenched in residential housing practices. While the stated intent of the Act was to reform these racist policies, it proved hollow, as it was not only poorly enforced but also failed to undo the effects of the previous policies.

Institutional racism—"the differential access to resources and opportunities by race, policies, laws, and practices that reinforce racial inequity" (Mendez et al., 2012, p. 1)—takes many forms and has often been accompanied by legislative policies such as the ones I mentioned, and sadly it continues to be passed down through generations. Additionally, redlining segregation systemically worked to separate races and remove resources from Black communities, concentrating poverty there and centralizing wealth in White communities (Massey & Denton, 1993). Wealth is defined as the difference between a family's gross assets and their liabilities. When looking at families by race, White families have the highest level of wealth by both mean (average amount within group) and median (the typical household within group). One of the most efficient ways to accumulate wealth is through homeownership and passing down of property through generations. However, the unwillingness of the Federal Housing Administration to guarantee loans to

Black families meant that 98 percent of mortgage loans went to White families (NPR, 2018). Thus, Black families were left with only the possibility of renting, which hindered their ability to create generational wealth.

I wish I could tell you that this was the end, but candidly it's very much the beginning. For example, you might wonder where these Black families ended up having to live. As a result of these redlining practices, families of color, especially Black families, were forced to live in homes with toxic lead-based paints, closer to industrial plants, and farther from places with fresh food and clean water. Research suggests that living close to these facilities is linked to adverse health outcomes (Brender et al., 2011), such as pregnancy complications that include central nervous system defects, renal dysplasia, congenital heart defects, chromosomal anomalies, and fetal death. In addition, such neighborhoods also have higher rates of various childhood cancers such as leukemia, brain cancer, and lymphoma. Lastly, living near these facilities increases risk for asthma, hospitalizations, stroke, respiratory symptoms, and PCB toxicity ('The Color of Law' Details How U.S. Housing Policies Created Segregation, 2017).

While this book focuses on Black men, I do not think I could do the topic justice without also mentioning the injustices experienced by Black women. Pregnant Black women's experience of stress, discrimination, and poor neighborhood quality increased the likelihood that their babies would be born prematurely—that is, at less than thirty-seven weeks' gestation. Preterm birth is the leading cause of infant mortality in the United States. Moreover, there are racial disparities in birth outcomes, in that Black women in the United States are almost two times more likely than White women to have their infants die and or to deliver preterm. Considering these variables, the data and research suggest that institutional racism, through redlining, may be a significant factor in the racial and ethnic disparities in preterm birth. It is important to note that the complexity of preterm birth is an interaction between factors at the individual, family, community, and society levels (Hogan & Ferre, 2001).

We know that many Black families continue to live in these systemically under-resourced and infrastructurally deficit areas. Consequently, it is no surprise that these Black families, facing a lack of health care resources, suffered far greater than other groups with their community's storage and dissemination of health care resources while contending with the COVID-19 pandemic (National Academies of Sciences, Engineering and Medicine, 2020; Schmidt et al., 2021).

It's funny, I remember being taught about the Great Depression during history class, which was one of my favorites. I found it fascinating to know the tales of the past and the remarkable individuals who walked this earth just like I do. While the details of the lessons have since faded, I remember being taught about Franklin Delano Roosevelt's

New Deal as a genius idea that saved us all from financial despair. However, the rest was not included. . . .

A Tale of Life Lessons

> When I was in high school, Marvin, a friend of mine, was trying to complete a homework assignment related to science. So, at fourteen I took my bright green three-speed English Racer bicycle my mother bought me from east Baltimore City, where we lived, to a park in a nearby county. . . . Anyway, we reached the park, which was in a practically all-White neighborhood, and proceeded to an area in the park where a stream was flowing. From a distance, suddenly, we heard people calling us names. They couldn't have been talking to anyone else, as we were the only Blacks around . . . derogatory names or meant to be interpreted as such, like Black boy, Bwana, and other words I don't recall. There was a lot of yelling. Thinking back and knowing now what Bwana means, I don't think they knew the word means boss . . . and I don't think they felt that way. Anyhow, most of them gathered and started walking towards Marvin and I. They had been playing baseball until we arrived. So, some of them started hurling rocks at us. Marvin and I had no choice but to take our bikes in a hurry and walk with our bikes across the

> stream, which was deep enough to slow us down I recall. Marvin was hit in his side by a rock. When we got to the other side, an old lady appeared who helped us. The police came and Marvin and I identified some of the individuals to the police officers as we headed away from the scene. I don't think the police cared much and were ignoring us; it felt like they were mainly interested in seeing us head back to the city, *where we belonged* . . . (yuk yuk). So, they escorted us from their police car until we were safely out of the area. For a time after this, Marvin and I talked about this incident and sometimes were able to find laughter. I never forgot that as you can see. It was a good lesson though. I am sure I became more sensitive to my surroundings and ultimately a better person as a result.

Reflecting on stories like this from my dad's childhood—which took place toward the end of the redlining from a policy standpoint—were a part of how I developed the topic of this book. Quick adaptations made in and from acts of injustice highlight the resilience of the Black community. He immediately learned who he could and could not rely on, how to assess a dangerous situation, and, lastly, how to use humor to preserve his well-being after the incident. As we think about generations of Black families—and particularly Black men—that have contended with these obstacles, it is imperative we understand the impact these events have had on their well-being. Black men must contend with various adversities, such as daily acts of interpersonal and systemic racism. Yet Black Americans continue to display strong coping strategies and resilience in the face of trauma (Milner, 2020). Through stories like my father's, we can understand the development of resilience and social well-being. His story exemplifies existing research on how Black men continue to rise through a commitment to learning from hardship, creative supportive environments, and reflecting/refocusing (Teti et al., 2012). Moreover, seminal research underscores the development of these strategies by examining Black culture in the family system, specifically noting the development of resilient children, steadfast optimism, elastic households, and kin-structured networks (Hall & King, 1982). Understanding the stories of resilience through trauma and strife is important to truly grasp the experiences of Black men.

"Whitey on the Moon"

After the United States invested the equivalent of $280 billion (in 2022 dollars) in the Apollo program, artist Gil Scott-Heron responded by releasing his 1970 spoken word poem, "Whitey on the Moon," to protest systemic racism in the United States expressed through economic and public health discrimination. Through his words he artistically exposed the absurdity and disrespect America displayed by endeavoring in a race to the moon while simultaneously strangling Black communities.

Today, over fifty years later, we see both the historic effects of the devaluation of Black communities and current inequities. For instance, access to adequate health care and healthy living environments is blocked for many Black Americans by discriminatory housing practices (Zonta, 2019). Housing market discrimination is sometimes disguised through family and or individual socio-economic status (SES) in order to push legislation and policy. The more I studied this, the more I've come to consider this to be weaponized SES. What I mean by this is that once federal housing laws stated that it was illegal to discriminate on the basis of skin color, many systems, such as our housing industries, used SES as a weapon to discriminate against people of color instead. Knowing that because of historical economic racism Black people did not have access to the wealth that White families did, housing agencies blocked Black people from housing opportunities in areas rich in resources through economic discrimination that shielded the institutions from accusations of racism.

SES matters. White families, on average, have eight times the wealth of Black families (Bhutta et al., 2019). Further, Black Americans are 1.8 times more likely to experience poverty. Black families have the lowest household income by race, and Black men in particular are more likely than members of other groups to live in poverty and lack adequate health care (U.S. Census Bureau, 2021). Further, it is important to me both that I share with you and that you understand the impact of weaponized SES on our bodies. Multiple researchers have specifically explored how a person's SES impacts their brain's functioning and development (Buckley et al., 2019). And the research clearly suggests that SES can influence how a person's brain activates, specifically in the areas of the brain designed for cognitive and behavioral tasks, and can lead to differences in the size of the hippocampus and amygdala.

Let me be clear, this does not suggest that people with more money have an innate cognitive superiority over people of lower SES—à la the doctrine of white supremacy. However, it does allude to two things: First, by experiencing the stress of poverty, a person's brain will wire itself in a way that is most functional under the conditions of poverty rather than in a way that would be most functional for wealthier conditions. Essentially, brains will adapt to their environment in a way that seems most helpful for surviving those circumstances. In this regard, navigating the conditions of poverty requires intelligence. Recognizing this allows us to see people's struggle as linked to their environmental conditions rather than mistakenly identifying it as a generational, biological deficiency. In conjunction with this is a second piece: having access to resources provides additional benefits, including more brain synapses. We must fully understand that this does not imply deficiency; rather, it points to the consequences created by various forms of discrimination, as people with higher SES have access to resources that allow for healthier development of their brains.

In the discourse regarding the impact of institutional racism on the Black community, the effects of discriminatory housing practices are seldom mentioned, let alone the extent to which they continue to shape the Black community and America as a whole. Considering the negative effects on health and well-being in poor neighborhoods, we must include this in our understanding of racism (Duncan and Kawachi, 2018; Krieger, 2011). The impact of housing discrimination in communities continues. When comparing the aftermath of foreclosures following the Great Depression of 1929 and the Great Recession of 2008, researchers uncovered significant differences between Black communities and White communities (McClure et al., 2018). For example, White individuals recovered from foreclosure at a significantly higher rate than Black individuals as a result of current and historic policies that provided and continue to provide White people with advantages. It would be an inadequate process to only examine policies within the health-care system as a result of centuries of no justice for majority Black communities. This vacuum approach will only further dilute the experiences of Black men and America's inept approaches to right its wrongs. It is imperative that historical perspective and context be included in discussions.

Generationally Established Side Effects

As previously stated, the obstacles posed by systemic social injustice appear unending, and the side effects Black men develop to maintain a sense of self are often painful. In her book *Post Traumatic Slave Syndrome: America's Legacy of Enduring Injury and Healing*, Dr. Joy Degruy outlines common psychological effects of generations of racism toward Black people that may be present in Black men who have experienced the twin pandemics. Post-traumatic slave syndrome (PTSS) is described as "a condition that exists when a population has experienced multigenerational trauma resulting from centuries of slavery and continues to experience oppression and institutionalized racism today. Added to this is a belief (real or imagined) that the benefits of the society in which they live are not accessible to them" (Degruy, 2017, p. 105). The three characteristics that embody PTSS are *vacant esteem*, *ever-present anger*, and *racist socialization.* Vacant esteem is an experience in which a person sees themselves as having little to no worth; it can be bolstered by consistent messages of inferiority from society, family, and community. Ever-present anger describes a continued experience of emotional anger (conscious or otherwise) as the result of ongoing degradation and systematic blocking of resources and opportunities. Racist socialization results from the insidious teaching of the *slave master's value system*, which imparts the belief that *whiteness* and all things white are superior and that all things Black are inferior. An example of this comes from an infamous figure in the miseducation of race, Carl Linnaeus. When describing the Black race, Linnaeus states they are "phlegmatic, cunning, lazy, lustful, careless and governed by caprice" (Degruy, 2017, p. 43). This raises three questions: First, do Black men need to resist this narrative or assimilate to it in order to defend their sense of self (Watson, 2013)? Second, in what ways has society adopted these negative narratives about Black men? Third, what derivatives of these narratives have been created in everyday life through explicit and implicit bias? For example, if Americans have adopted the belief that Black men are lazy, people who unconsciously or consciously adhere to this belief about Black men may more easily accept that Black suffering is the result of Black people's own laziness.

Rejected: Education on Racism

Attempts to undo miseducation for the next generation have been met with fervent opposition. For example, critical race theory (CRT) has experienced heavy scrutiny during this time (Vock, 2021) because of a misplaced concern that it teaches White children to dislike themselves for being White. Some media outlets referenced cases of White children being "ashamed" for being White; however, local reporters were unable to find evidence of these stated cases (Vock, 2021). What CRT does do, instead, is break down what racism is and how it functions in a given society; additionally, it explicates the emotional and psychological experiences of the people victimized by racism (Valdes et al., 2002). Johnson-Ahorlu (2017) conceptualized how CRT can create a powerful structure and understanding for activists who work toward dismantling unjust systems, laying out possible social movement strategies and research designs. Using CRT in education can be an effective way to proactively dismantle racist systems by educating future generations about racism and its continued history. However, opposition to critical education on racism and its continued impact on Black men means that their experience goes unvalidated and institutional racism goes uncorrected.

While social injustice toward the Black community dates back centuries, starting in 2020 the COVID-19 pandemic forced the United States to slow down and reckon with its racism as social injustice after social injustice were paraded by media outlets.

A Comment of Perspective

"You gotta understand, a pandemic is just one more thing for us. There's a lot of pandemics for niggas," Michael Che stated in partial jest on his sketch comedy show, *That Damn Michael Che*, before telling a story of losing his friend to gun violence during the COVID-19 pandemic. The obstacles Black men face in the United States appear endless, yet they have continued to find creative means to survive systemic suffering. While Che's show is comedic, these statements illustrate how Black men have had to continually and routinely contend with traumatic events through generations. One could even say that the past few years held two pandemics for Black men, both holding legitimate risk to the loss of life. Despite this, Black men have displayed resilience on small and large stages, including professional sports and national activism (*Color of Change*, 2021; Galily, 2021). This book examines just how Black men have cultivated resilience and well-being during the global COVID-19 health pandemic while managing the continued pandemic of racial injustice.

2

A Story of Black Public Health

Nashville Area Black male House Supervisor—

R: I'm a methodical guy, I don't get in a hurry. When you're a methodical, laid-back Black man, a lot of people think that that's a weakness. And it's not, it's an incredible strength. I was a house supervisor at a hospital the day of the Christmas day bombing, and we only had two working phones in the entire hospital. And so, I was able to keep the entire hospital rolling and kept the entire hospital calm. . . . I always say my goal is to keep the waters calm; if the waters are calm, people work better. But then some people at the job they complain, "Well, [name] is too laid back." That was part of my evaluation, I was dinged, really badly. The chief nursing officer said, "Well, they say you're not assertive." I say, "What do you want, an angry black man walking down the hospital?" And this was around the time of the

George Floyd protests. . . . He looked at me. I said, "You know the environment we're working in, what do you want?" I said, "Lemme give you an example, do you know someone escaped from the hospital the other day?" He said, "Really?!" I said, "You know why you didn't know? Because we got him back and nobody was harmed; the team is safe. It's because I was here." He looked at me and he said, "Wow." That's what me being a methodical person gets you.

M: Here you are . . . in the hospital setting (R: Right.) got a whole pandemic happening (R: Right.). A bomb goes off. What is perhaps your greatest strength is being re-narrated as a liability.

R: Right.

For me, it's always felt like a fluctuating force of push and pull riddles our public health history. If you're wanting to pinpoint a *bad* time in comparison to a *good* time in American history, you'll quickly realize, as I once did, how impossible it is. Moreover, when it comes to public health for Black Americans, the more we learn the more we come to realize the main reason there were even moments of good was because of the resilient and creative efforts of Black people.

Beginning in the late nineteenth century, Black physicians, activists, and scientists became concerned about health inequalities between Black people and White people, such as higher rates of infectious disease and higher rates of maternal and infant mortality (Brown, 1937; National Negro Health Week, n.d.). At the time there existed a narrative of Black biological inferiority that had been around since slavery—in fact, it was one of the ideas leveraged as a reason not to end slavery. Essentially, the intent of the idea was to instill in the population a belief that Black people would die off without the *benefits* of being slaves. The people who espoused this narrative stated that the increase in disease among Black people was evidence of inferiority and of Black people's inability to survive without being enslaved. However, leaders of the Black health movement shook off ideas of Black dependency and invested in finding the real causes of health inequality. These scholars came to the conclusion that continues to ring true today: racism. Though they did not use today's language of systemic structural oppression, these leaders were already hitting on many variables we discuss today, over a century later.

Instead of focusing on biological inferiority as the cause of health inequalities, scholars urged our country to focus on variables such as discrimination in environment, housing, and living conditions. Their research efforts sparked local movements that worked to address health issues within their communities. One of Booker T. Washington's last projects,

National Negro Health Week (NNHW), was perhaps the zenith of their work. He and other Black leaders were aware of the lack of concern for Black health within the country. This lack of concern was highlighted by the difference in life expectancy between White people (low to mid-fifties) and Black people (mid-thirties). These Black leaders focused their attention on health promotion and programing (Pollitt, 1996); enter NNHW. Cities that agreed to observe NNHW would receive a number of benefits, including education, community support, improved sanitation, and health exams. This sustained creativity in the face of adversity led to the establishment of the Office of Negro Health in the early 1920s.

However, as I said, it's not that clean-cut. Sandwiched between these efforts were atrocities such as the Tuskegee experiments. Beginning in 1932, this infamous study sought to look at untreated syphilis in Black men. The researchers lied to poor, often illiterate Black men in Tuskegee, Alabama—considered the "black belt" for its large number of Black sharecroppers—about the purpose of the study, saying that the men would be treated for "bad blood," a term used to refer to the presence of various symptoms and illnesses such as fatigue, anemia, and syphilis. However, the researchers did not provide treatment for syphilis, despite the health problems, such as blindness and dementia, caused by the disease. Instead, only placebos, such as aspirin, were administered. In addition to failing to treat the men for syphilis, researchers actively found ways to ensure they could not receive treatment elsewhere. For example, the researchers contacted county health departments with a list of participants' names so they would not treat them. After the participants died, their bodies were examined for scientific discovery. While penicillin, the cure for syphilis, was later discovered in 1947, it was withheld from all the participants until a New York and Washington news report broke the story in 1972. It is unknown just how many men, women, and children were infected with the disease over the forty-year history of the Tuskegee experiments. What should be emphasized here is that this was not an independent study; rather, the Tuskegee study was done in conjunction with the United States Public Health Service. Stories of such events are passed down from generation to generation in Black families, creating ongoing and justifiable doubt about our health care systems.

Psychological Distress

I decided in 2018 to move from just outside Philadelphia to Kansas in order to pursue a doctorate. As a former collegiate athlete, albeit washed-up, I would often run to take care of my mind and body. As a Black man, whenever I move it always takes some time in a new place—especially some place like Kansas—before the cognitive energy I spend examining if my environment is accepting of me can dissipate and begin to bloom into a feeling of safety. And when Ahmaud Arbery's murder came across my TV, my protective instincts returned, but this time in the form of memories my brain told me I needed to remember in order to feel safe. It was like an alarm clock waking me up from a daydreamed sense of security I could not risk having. When I embraced my feelings, I realized Ahmaud's murder made me question the people around me and whether I could rely on them. Though it's hard for me to say, it even met me in my dreams, as an all-too-real nightmare of jogging in the park at night before being turned around by an older White man pointing his gun six inches from my sternum.

As a result of the brain's mirror neurons, retraumatization can take place when an individual views media that reminds them of emotionally jarring experiences they have had or vicarious traumas. This raises a question about the psychological impact Black men have experienced while seeing Black Americans beaten and killed by both police and White citizens, in addition to seeing protests for Black rights continually discredited by high-ranking government officials. Seeing Black Americans beaten and killed can also evoke vicarious grief, defined as "the experience of loss and consequent grief/mourning that occurs following the deaths of others not personally known by the mourner" (Rando, 1997, p. 259). When we experience vicarious grief, we grieve not only for the mourners but also for those who passed. The losses reactivate our own grieving even though we are unconnected to the one who was lost. One factor that influences vicarious grieving is the amount of psychological separation between an individual and the mourner. The more an individual shares the same identifying information as the individual mourning or the individual who has passed (e.g., race, ethnicity, gender, family circumstance, and age), the greater the likelihood of vicarious grieving. With this in mind, Black men, continually being bombarded with the death of people who look like them, may trigger retraumatization and may grieve for themselves and those sharing similar racial and ethnic backgrounds.

We have seen how national and worldwide disasters can affect individuals psychologically, for example generating anxiety, depression, and symptoms of post-traumatic stress disorder (PTSD). This was certainly true during the COVID-19 pandemic, when rates of such symptoms increased drastically, in some instances tenfold, from the prior year. Mandatory social distancing and quarantine measures reduced the number of COVID-19 cases, but prolonged quarantine has been shown to increase depressive symptoms and have adverse effects on individual well-being (Brooks et al., 2020). Some studies have examined the effectiveness of defense mechanisms and mindfulness for coping with psychological distress from COVID-19. Further, in an effort to predict distress during the COVID-19 pandemic, research found that adverse childhood experiences led to more limited use of coping strategies, which in turn led to greater psychological distress. In many instances, the Black community has found strength and resilience through collective activities (Degruy, 2014; Du Bois, 1903), yet such activities were limited by measures to reduce the spread of COVID-19. As we transition into discussing the COVID-19 pandemic as well as my sit-down interviews with Black men, it is important we keep in mind the dynamic happening between defense mechanism and psychological distress.

COVID-19 Pandemic

When the pandemic first reached global status, research entities, communities, and individuals quickly recognized and called for research to understand its effects. Significant symptoms of trauma were noted among high school students in China at the beginning of the pandemic, including sleep disorders, emotional difficulties, loneliness, depression, and anxiety (Gusau et al., 2020). Scholars in Wuhan, China, examined how resilience and positive emotions could potentially protect from some of these symptoms (Yang et al., 2020). Research has well documented how psychological trauma can be a negative predictor of well-being; however, resilience and positive emotion serve to mediate the relationship between trauma and well-being. I asked myself if Black men have been able to maintain resilience and positivity in the face of the added psychological trauma of social injustices? Once again, the answers were not that clean cut.

COVID-19 impacted everyone's lives in ways extending from the micro to the macro: individual health concerns, family health concerns, community management, governmental action, and global reactions. While I was examining health care resources during the COVID-19 pandemic within the United States, I found that even well-intended assistance continued to fall short of equitable distribution of resources, with Black people receiving the short end of the stick. Moreover, battling in the arena of America—marked by historical inequities in every system—Black men were not only contending with COVID-19 difficulties, but doing so while broadcast messages of racial injustices toward their same-race peers were covered by news outlets and seeped into their own lives.

Infections and Vaccinations

Treadwell (2020) comprehensively examined the effects of COVID-19 on Black Americans. The Black community has been disproportionately affected by COVID-19, and Black men even more so (Wortham et al., 2020). Early in the pandemic, for example, Black men were dying at twice the rate of their White male peers (Ayoubkhani et al., 2020), and Black Americans were dying from COVID-19 at three times the rate of the rest of the population. These disparities continued even years into the pandemic. In fact, as virus variants emerged, so did increases in racial disparities. Black men had among the lowest vaccination rates in the midst of the pandemic. At one point during my exploration, White Americans made up 82 percent of COVID-19 cases and 92 percent of vaccinations in the United States. In contrast, Black Americans were 14 percent of cases and only 3 percent of vaccinations (Ndugga, 2021). Looking deeper provides the reasons for this trend.

Even in states that were working to distribute the vaccine equitably struggled to do so (Ndugga, 2021). A quick google search could tell you a host of reasons for this. For example, Black men are much more likely to be "essential workers"—people critical to our infrastructure. They are also more likely to be in tighter living conditions, to have less access to health care, to experience chronic health conditions, and to have higher levels of stress, which is linked to decreases in our immune system. However, if we were to look at this in a vacuum we would be doing serious harm by knowingly or otherwise perpetuating a narrative of Black inferiority from the micro level of their biology to the macro level of community; just as the nineteenth-century leaders highlighted, these problems of inequality are systemic. Black men's hesitancy to get vaccinated is in large part a psychological product of experiences and stories of systemic oppression, such as the Tuskegee experiments, which have led Black men not to trust the government (Brandon et al., 2013). In addition, many Black men still live in areas that do not have adequate sites for vaccine storage and distribution (Reverby, 2021). These structural problems within the community are again linked to histories of racism through redlining and continued underfunding, as referenced in the previous chapters (Hogan & Ferre, 2001; Mendez et al., 2012).

As I tuned into the news during this pandemic, I had to watch politicians and journalists discuss in a confused frenzy how Black communities—which are really areas with mostly Black residents that were originally created through redlining—had trouble getting vaccines into the community, storing them, and distributing them. I needed to find equanimity in my rage and desire to be understood in those moments not only so I could find internal peace, but also so I could properly articulate my thoughts. If you were shocked and angered by the vaccine problems, know that it is OK to feel this way, but it is not helpful to stay in this state. The neighborhoods Black Americans were forced to live in were never designed to have the structural capabilities to house or distribute these resources, and they were not supported in gaining these capabilities. In short, they were designed to fail the people who lived within their lines. Generations of discriminatory housing practices have increased chronic health problems, and the holistic phenomenological experience of oppression has increased stress in Black men, which makes them more susceptible to COVID-19. Initial research on the pandemic showed that poverty, lack of health care services, and inadequate health insurance increase the potential to have negative effects from contracting COVID-19.

Few people discuss how physical health can be influenced by societal factors (Assari, 2018) that do not pertain to the health sector (Commission on Social Determinants of Health, 2008). Thus, the gap in health between Black and White Americans in many ways even predates health care disparities. There is a twofold process that leads to this gap. The first element is "differential exposure," which refers to the fact that Black Americans have statistically less access to resources such as well-paying jobs, job opportunities, and quality education while having increased exposure to risk factors including discrimination. The second element is "diminished gains," which refers to the decreased health benefits from psychological and socioeconomic resources that lead Black Americans to experience fewer positive outcomes from the assets and benefits they already possess in comparison to White Americans. For example, employment has been shown to be a greater protective factor for White Americans than for Black Americans. This holds true for education as well. There are many reasons for diminished gains, including labor market preferences and practices, differences in income and wealth generation and purchasing power, cumulative gains for White people based on initial advantage; and the extra cost associated with upward social mobility among Black Americans. While these concepts in and of themselves are meaningful to explore, I cannot belabor them here. Instead, I will focus on the pattern of individual and systemic discrimination that is a binding element within these variables.

Research outlines three paths by which racial bias can lead to disparities in health care (Penner et al., 2014): (1) the psychological and physical impact of discrimination, (2) the implicit bias of physicians, and (3) a breakdown in communication between patient and physician as a result of physicians' implicit bias. This highlights the importance of implementing culturally sensitive policies to reduce these biases, such as physician-focused approaches that require additional courses that teach soon-to-be-clinicians about racial health disparities using a systemic lens while addressing their own biases, patient-focused approaches such as values affirmations to mitigate stereotype threat, and approaches designed to create effective communication in physician-patient relations by building trust. However, without these adjustments being made, what was surviving the pandemic like given the disparity in health care services, where Black men continue to suffer differential treatment?

"Containment and control, that's what they are doing, that's what they want to keep doing." The words of my father speak to the keen awareness of some Black men who are able to see the systemic cogs working. Other individuals within communities that are mostly Black appear to be aware of the disproportionate distribution of resources across communities within the United States, specifically in comparison to White communities as well. Members of Black communities see a direct link between the discriminatory response to the COVID-19 pandemic and the national HIV/AIDS pandemic. In other words, the system has done this before. Further, prisons, jails, and detention centers have alarmingly high rates of COVID-19, with reported rates of infection of close to 80 percent of the population, and these rates are likely underreported. This is worth noting because the United States boasts the highest rates of incarceration in the world, with Black men having the highest likelihood of being incarcerated at 28 percent over their lifetime. Black men are also incarcerated at nearly triple the rate of other groups: despite accounting for only 12 percent of the U.S. population, they account for approximately 33 percent of all incarcerated people in the United States.

Distrust in Government

When I first went to write this section I had to hold back laughter. I thought to myself, do I really need to tell you why Black men don't trust the government? I can't help but think about iconic jokes from my childhood watching *Chappelle's Show* or the *Boondocks'* artful satire to expose the relationship between Black people and the United States government. And yet, I couldn't shake the feeling that I still needed to include this section. As a therapist, I know that my generational pain, resentment, and annoyance find refuge in humor, and that it is important to share my experience. I'm thankful for the safe haven given by Black comedians because during this twin-pandemic I especially noticed a resurgence of these feelings. It came from what felt like a comparison between pains. Some White people espoused a belief that they were being oppressed, and that filled me with a rage I didn't know I could experience. I heard complaints from White people on all sides of the sociopolitical aisle upset they weren't getting what they wanted. Some said things like, "White men are the ones really being oppressed." Others talked to me about how they know Black men experience racism, but in the same breath, using a passive-aggressive tactic, they'd talk to me about how hard they had to work to get to where they are. It's been over two and a half decades, yet Chris Rock's 1996 stand-up, *Bring the Pain*, finds a comfortable space in my head: "The White man thinks he's losing the Country. . . . Shut the f*** up, White people ain't losing s***. If y'all losing, whose winning? It ain't us!" So while I laugh, please know that there is so much more I need you to be able to see. Sometimes I just need to laugh so I can smile and not "go upside your head," as my mom would say. Now let's dive in.

The exploitation of Henrietta Lacks's body in 1951, the avoidance and then failed investigations into Emmett Till's murder in 1955,[1] Jim Crow laws until 1965, FBI surveillance of civil rights and Black Power movement leaders, and countless massacres (such as Bloody Sunday) that would not conclude until 1968—the same year as Dr. King's assassination—all while redlining practices were devastating

[1] Carolyn Bryant Donham, who accused Till, was not arrested because, per a 2022 CBS News report, the Leflore County sheriff at the time did not want to "bother" her.

Black wealth. It should be no surprise that many Black Americans do not trust in the United States government. With distrust in government comes distrust in vaccinations. Low vaccination rates in Black communities extend beyond COVID-19, as historically low numbers of Black Americans are vaccinated for influenza each year. This has left many Black communities feeling, at best, neglected by government action and, at worst, victimized by violations of the four core ethical principles involved in clinical trials: beneficence, nonmaleficence, justice, and autonomy.

As we expand to other historic health crises, we see similar trends, such as Black men living in low SES areas needing to find creative resilience strategies during the HIV pandemic, as they did not trust in the government's ability to provide safe and effective support. In essence, Black men knew their own resilience strategies would provide better outcomes for themselves and their communities than the government's strategies would.

3

Tightroping Resilience and Well-Being

Sittin' here restin' my bones
And this loneliness won't leave me alone, listen
Two thousand miles, I roam
Just to make this dock my home
Now I'm just gon' sit, at the dock of the bay
Watchin' the tide roll away, ooh yeah
Sittin' on the dock of the bay
Wastin' time
[Harmonic whistling]
(Otis Redding, 1968)

Back in college I did a million things. I was coming off thirteen years of academic underperformance. A result of my American miseducation, where people of my skin were guided directly or indirectly away from any scholastic achievement. However, going into college I was determined to change that. While there was a ton of catching up I needed to do, in those four years I like to think I did more than just make up for lost time. During my undergraduate program I was a Division I athlete, resident assistant, advisor on multiple clubs, and a full-time student. It was difficult, and probably way too much, but I pushed myself. Most days I started at 5:30am for weightlifting. Most nights I finished around 11:00pm, with few breaks in between except for food.

If I'm being honest, others probably could have done my day faster, as it often takes me longer to learn things than most. I've always been a bit jealous of people like my brothers who could read and grasp concepts quickly. For me, ten pages in an hour is a good day. Needless to say, I spent a lot of time in the library. Almost every night during the work week and most weekend mornings—when I didn't have a track meet—I was in the library. Even when my body was tired, I went until my mind had worked equally as hard. Making sure I took small five- to ten-minute breathers that included some of my favorite songs for motivation, I was absolutely determined. I thought to myself: if I grind hard enough, it will get better.

And so, I sat. With my almost ritualistic pattern anyone could find me—first floor back right table meant for groups—usually alone, but with the occasional passing friend. I'd be dying in there trying to read and understand texts like Martin Heidegger's Zollicon Seminars, Thomas Hobbes's *Leviathan*, or literally anything that involved math. But, for four years, at the end of my night as I was walking back from the library I would queue, on my iPod Nano, Otis Redding's "(Sittin' On) the Dock of the Bay." A song about our continual attempts to find beauty through struggle and misfortune. It just felt right. On my slow stroll to my dorm, I often had a smile of satisfaction while my head wandered into the clouds. I was proud of myself. Young, Black, and (getting) educated, I could envision myself making a difference one day.

Music has always helped me to dream or connect, and almost a decade later my wandering mind remains, but with new images. In fact, since I began writing this for you, I started picturing my resilience and well-being as two people dancing in a crowded room. The ones where you're elbow to elbow with people and smells you can't recognize, and the drink that spilled an hour ago has long since turned into a sticky adhesive now on the bottom of your favorite shoes. In my daydreams during the twin-pandemic I couldn't help but see how some days the beat of the world was easier to find and move with while other days it was like trying to anticipate the right move to a bebop track. No matter what you do, you're going to get roughed up along the way. So as a Black man, you better keep it moving!

***

Did you know that resilience was once considered a bad thing in my field of psychology? While studying children in disadvantaged situations, psychologists concluded that developing or showing resilience during a time of adversity was problematic. Yes, when our field first started, looking at our ability to be resilient we thought it was dysfunctional for a person to be resilient when experiencing adversity. It was considered a dysfunctional denial of reality to show resilience (Hobfoll, 2002). When we look back at research like this, it is important to look at the cultural context in which it was written in order to understand it and avoid repeating its mistakes. Considering the researchers and the population studied, the results were no doubt connected to the unprocessed biases of my psychology predecessors. They continued to perpetuate a narrative of inferiority by placing themselves above those who were in disadvantaged positions. Examples such as this shows us how biases become harms in everyday people's lives.

Fortunately, in the 1990s we questioned how we were understanding what it meant to be human, and decided we needed to respect a person's competence and ability to adapt while also listing the potential effects of adversity on individuals and groups. By doing this, resilience was becoming conceptualized as a normal process of adaptation to extraordinary conditions, and in some instances an example of growth after traumatic events (Tedeschi & Calhoun, 2004). However, decades later we are still trying to fully understand the complexities of the web we created, such as how "good schools," money, social capital, and human capital influence positive development from a policy, community, education, family, and individual standpoint. In this, there exists a sort of dance between the adversity a person faces and how they can try to leverage their assets to overcome their situations.

What Is Resilience?

Psychologically, resilience is a multidimensional term with three separate orientations: *trait*, the personality characteristics that protect against adversity; *outcome*, the development of resilience after adversity; and *process*, a dynamic interaction of development and recuperation (Fergus & Zimmerman, 2005; Oshio et al., 2018). Multiple definitions of resilience have been posed through the years, such as "the ability to sustain competence under pressure and the capacity to recover from trauma" (Masten, 1994, p. 5) and "the capacity of a system to anticipate, adapt, and reorganize itself under conditions of adversity in ways that promote sustain its successful functioning" (Ungar, 2011, p. 127). Essentially, it is best characterized by the interaction between an individual and their outer spheres of interaction—in other words, an interaction between the micro and the macro.

However, it's important that we understand the potential cultural impact of traditional masculine norms on how these definitions came to define resilience. All of these definitions describe resilience in a way that paints a picture of a stout response to adversity, where the individual stands tall and moves forward without error or doubt. However, as a supervisor once told me, "Sometimes resilience looks like curling up in a ball." Our bodies and minds have a beautiful ability to adapt, and at the same time, it would be disrespectful to ourselves and the experiences of others for us to forget the pain that sits quietly in the lion hearts of those being resilient. They, like all of us, have moments of forlorn hope that sometimes look ugly, as they should. The fugue of emotions that can accompany us as a part of living in this world should be acknowledged. This may be important in understanding the contextual experience of Black men who, like all of us, influence and are influenced by their ecosystems. The pandemic, which was traumatic in itself, slowed the world down, and we as a country were subjected to more instances of racism in our own lives and we more frequently saw racism affect the lives of others.

Resilience in Action

"It's amazing why we keep loving this country, and this country does not love us back," I heard Head Coach Doc Rivers say in a 2020 press conference while fighting back tears in response to the continued violence against Black Americans. As the coach alluded to, many Black men in this country have a complex relationship with the United States; however, this has not stopped them from pursuing change in the country they love. For example, at the height of COVID-19, the NBA postponed play for a brief period. And not soon after beginning again in a quarantined bubble, another Black death was covered by the national news. In protest against the shooting of Jacob Blake, the players refused to play. In the months that followed the start of the pandemic, more Black men were killed by police officers and through acts of civil racism, in cases such as Ahmaud Arbery. While reckoning with a pandemic, the NBA supported its predominantly Black American player population by voicing their protest against the killings of Black Americans and police violence. This is not novel. Athletics throughout time have served as a mesh point in which the inequalities of society are challenged (Coop et al., 2019), and Black American athletes such as Muhammad Ali, Bill Russell, Tommie Smith, John Carlos, and Colin Kaepernick have, for decades, used creative strategies of resilience to inspire positive social change despite public and systematic chastisement. Seeing people in our community use their own resilience to engage in large-scale efforts for equality and justice can have a contagious effect. In this way, we work to bolster each other, ourselves, and our communities.

Further, by doing this we are very much teaching people how to be resilient while standing with them. Black men have continually shown that despite being subjected to systemic suffering, they have a propensity to adapt to adversity in order to survive. However, it is important that we try, as best we can, to nondualistically acknowledge their experience. By this I mean that it's important to avoid pushing the myopic narrative of "bootstrap" thinking in which an individual can overcome systemic barriers simply by grit alone. Instead, we should support a conceptualization of resilience based on strengths that puts into perspective broad ecological factors and individual competencies.

Additionally, it is important to ask ourselves what happens to a person after they have had to be resilient for so long. Oftentimes, they may need to recover from the traumatic events. Recovery has been considered a return to baseline functioning after the traumatic experiences that created the acute distress. As I began to think about this, my mind started to wander into the future. . . . I was anxious, and could feel the impact of yet-to-be-spoken words from popular platforms discussing how we finally *recovered* from the pandemic. I'm worried that our country will be quick to pat itself on the back, as it often does, and move on. However, it would be foolish to believe the end of COVID-19 is the end of a centuries-long American pandemic. If we look at the history of racism and the passing down of it generationally, this definition of recovery does not fit the circumstances of Black men. For example, right now as I sit here writing this, Black men are experiencing the immediate and indirect traumas of systemic injustice against Black people and public denials of their struggles, in addition to the stranglehold COVID-19 has placed on all of us, but with added obstacles again for Black men because of discrimination in health care. So when the COVID-19 pandemic ends, and we return to our supposed "baseline functioning," it is not accurate to assume that Black men have "recovered" when prior discrimination continues, and their wounds are still fresh.

Well-Being

The elusive concept of well-being is something that we humans have tried through centuries to pin down. And that makes sense: I mean how does one find the "right" words to convey the subjective experience of what it means to be a well (living) being? In our brief walk through history let's talk about three ways we, in the West, have tried to capture well-being: the pathogenic, the salutogenic, and the complete state models (Keyes, 2007). The pathogenic understanding—taken from the Greek word *pathos*, which means suffering—was adopted by my field in our earlier days when the idea of health was defined by the absence of disease or negative symptoms (Keyes, 2007). This essentially meant that we considered you to be "well" if you didn't have anything "wrong" with you. Next came the salutogenic approach, which focused more on the presence of *positive states* of feeling, functioning, and behavior (Strümpfer, 1995). Third is the complete state approach, which has been a well-regarded model of health in contemporary psychology. It refers to the complete presence of positive states of human functioning, in addition to the absence of negative symptoms (Keyes, 2007). This suggests that we can actually experience lower levels of distress in life and still not feel well—for example, "You know, Doc, my nightmares have gone away, but I still just don't feel good." This definition considers not only the sufferings a person is experiencing but also whether they are having positive experiences.

When a person experiences a complete state of well-being, we can consider them to be flourishing. This is when "an individual feels positive emotion toward life and is functioning well psychologically and socially." Further, "individuals diagnosed as flourishing have excellent emotional health, miss fewer days of work, cut back on work on fewer days, and have fewer physical limitations in their daily lives" (Keyes, 2003, p. 294). Some aspects of flourishing are easy, and we can savor them here and now; others are lifelong endeavors such as finding meaning. Culturally speaking, we can get to a place of flourishing in a myriad of ways, but regardless of how, when we do, we will function better.

As I was thinking about this, I wondered how familiar Black men are with trying to flourish while facing injustice. During this time I came across something interesting in my research journey: the Black, White paradox in health (Keyes, 2009). It told me that Black Americans had greater mental resilience when confronted with social inequality and discrimination than White Americans. The slight sense of pride I had in our collective ability to overcome was motivating. However, I knew an uncomplicated levity was not going to remain, because that is seldom the case. Predictably, I learned even more about the inevitable side effects that come from always having to be resilient, including higher rates of physical morbidity, which in turn increased the risk of mental distress. And that was just one of the byproducts of Black people's fight with injustice. However, I found myself thankful for what the researcher who identified the paradox did next.

If you're a researcher, you may have even predicted that he controlled for discrimination. If you're not, and don't know what this means, it may help to think about it this way: he used the information he gathered to create a fictious world where racism didn't exist. Then he checked to see what kind of lives Black people would have in that world. He found that Black Americans, in comparison to their White peers, showed an advantage in twelve of the thirteen signs of flourishing. In sum, Black Americans are finding ways to be resilient through social injustices; however, without these injustices they would have greater levels of well-being. We don't need to hit every marker to flourish, and over these last few years Black men have tried their best to find their moments of levity. So when shit hits the fan—for instance, "Doc, my old lady got COVID and white supremacists were marching down the street last week;[2] I'm worried about my kids!"— they still dig deep to find moments, here and now.

Black Masculine Identity and Well-Being: An Intersection

Sometime in the summer of 2020, I couldn't tell you when, but I decided to get funky. Quarantine was in full swing, and people of my skin color were being murdered so

---

[2] During the COVID-19 pandemic, even larger numbers of white supremacist activities took place.

regularly that my morning news felt predictable: someone Black died, and some White people, with an infrequent "token Black," were arguing over whether they should have died and whether their death was somehow justified. I was so fed up; I needed a moment of freedom filled with joy. So I danced. I remember walking out of my cramped bedroom and into the dining room, with hard wood floors perfect for sliding. I plugging my phone into the house stereo, opened up my soul music playlist, and did what any self-respecting person would do next by turning the volume up to max. The beat dropped right into my gut, and spread through my body, until I took shape. Led by the rhythm of James Brown's "The Payback," my two-step took me to the kitchen where I popped the top to a bottle of red. It was Apothic Red, which was just within a graduate student budget but still a taste Marley would be proud of. I got my groove on in the dining room to Aretha Franklin, Chaka Khan, Prince, and Lou Rawls, to name a few. Knowing I can't sing, and my mouth wide open no doubt failing to hit Lou's baritone, I thought to myself, "It's a good thing the volume is all the way up, I sound just like him." I can't remember how many songs I listened to by then, but at some point the table in the middle of the room was pushed out the way to make room for my attempt, though not the first in my life, to learn the Michael Jackson "Thriller" dance. Clearly visible through the French doors, my inhibitions rocked along to the beat as my demeanor said, "Passersby be damned, I'mma keep doing me." Candidly, I don't even remember if my roommates were home, and I really didn't care. By this point they were used to me, and I like to think they knew I needed this moment. The time was still, and filled with my smiles and laughs, as I forgot about the world for a brief moment . . .

Men in the United States are often socialized into a Eurocentric version of masculinity (Wester, 2013). In essence, White, middle-class, 1950s norms of what it means to be a man. However, forcing Black men into this model is linked to adverse psychological effects, such as decreased self-esteem and increased psychological distress (Mahalik, 2006). In short, the more Black men abide by American standards of masculinity, the lower their self-esteem and the higher their distress. If we understand history, this is not a surprising revelation. In her novel *We Real Cool: Black Men and Masculinity* bell hooks artistically canvasses the perverse socialization of Black men since they set foot on a plantation. In the confines of slavery, Black men were forcibly taught a new form of masculinity that required the domination of not only the female gender but every individual and system. Accounts taken at the time from Black men, both enslaved and free, outlined how they were broken into behaving *correctly* to satisfy the needs of white insecurity played out through what we incorrectly consider masculinity.

Centuries later we still find ourselves here. At the intersection of domination and submission, Black men are in many ways forced onto a hamster wheel and told to run in pursuit of an ideal that we cannot achieve, but are nonetheless compared to. I can tell you from my own experience and others' experiences how we are called lazy and offensive for any brand of swagger that does not live up to colonialized norms. Or laughed at for *being White* when we achieve success that doesn't fall within America's own racist archetype of what a Black man is *supposed to be.* This makes for a difficult coming-of-age experience for many Black men, who often describe some of their most difficult moments in life as happening during adolescence as they learn how their experience, because of the color of their skin, was different than their White peers. Many young Black men experience a double-bind. They can fight the uphill battle by not conforming, assuming they have the support around them to do so, to seek liberation. Or they can concede and slowly but painfully burn from the negative side effects that are to come, consciously or otherwise.

How Black men identify as men is significantly different than the way that White men identify as men. For Black men, masculinity is often multidimensional and defined through elements such as community, spirituality, family, humanism, accountability and responsibility, maturity, and self-awareness (Chaney, 2009; Hammond & Mattis, 2005; Hunter & Davis, 1992; Mincey et al., 2014). However, Black people face difficulties as a result of racially driven assaults on their sense of self (Hardy, 2016). Black men are more likely than White men to experience acts of discrimination based on race, and such events have been shown to have adverse effects on mental health (Pitcan, 2018; Bennett, 2004), with racial oppression consistently showing chronic psychosocial effects (Akbar, 1996; Jackson, 1990; Johnson, 1990). Despite this, the creativity of Black resilience persists. For example, using self-reinforcement in the face of racism decreased psychological distress and increased self-esteem. To be clear, this is not novel information, as it actually connects to decades of work from leaders in Black racial identity development such as William Cross and Janet Helms.

For decades, research fixated on understanding the Black experience in terms of negativity (Cross, 1994). Majority White scholars appeared to be trying to prove the point of Black inferiority. At the same time, vastly outnumbered Black leaders tried to combat this with their days in court (à la *Brown v. Board of Education*) and studies such as the Clark's "doll test" (Clark & Clark, 1950; Kendi, 2022). Black leaders were saying: we do not yearn to be you or be led by you; rather, we desire and are entitled to the resources and respect you give to yourselves for having white skin. Out of this, what would become the groundbreaking model of Black racial identity, originally referred to as "Nigrescence," was born in the 1970s. Its creator, William Cross, described this as a "phenomenological interpretation of the Negro-to-Black conversion experience" (1971, p. 14) because he believed there is a process Black Americans must go through to reject the "nigger" identity that was thrust on them and fully accept and embrace their own unique definition of Blackness. Or in the words of W. E. B. Du Bois, Black people must undergo the "oceanic" process of becoming "the New Negro" (Lewis, 1994).

Based much more in strengths than theories prior, Cross's model originally detailed five stages of Black identity development before being adjusted to four (Cross, 1991). The first stage, *Preencounter*, is when a Black person disowns their Blackness in an attempt to assimilate totally to White culture. In this stage many Black people may experience shame or a learned hopelessness that nothing they do will make a difference, and so they try to assimilate. Some Black people in this stage have sadly absorbed forms of miseducation from the slave master's doctrine, accepting either that they are lesser than because they are Black or seeing themselves as struggling because they are just not working as hard as others.

In the following stage, *Encounter*, a Black person experiences a significantly traumatic event that catapults them out of the first stage. This experience shatters their current framework and makes them challenge their previous perspectives regarding race. If you grew up watching *The Fresh Prince of Bel-Air*, the show provides a great example. When Will and Carlton are driving in a nice neighborhood in a nice car, without doing anything wrong, they were pulled over and arrested for stealing the car—which they had not done, as it was owned by Uncle Phil. Originally defending the officers for "just doing their jobs," Carlton is challenged by Will and Uncle Phil to see how their actions were actually racial profiling. As Will explains, "No map is going to save you, and neither is your glee club or your fancy Bel-Air address or who your daddy is. When you're driving in a nice car in a strange neighborhood, none of that matters." At this point, Carlton is left existentially uncertain as he realizes the world is not what he thought it was. Encounters are often a very traumatic process, as our entire understanding of who we are and our place in the world is shaken. Sometimes we additionally ask ourselves who we have been, and the answer to that question can potentially be painful.

The majority of Black people experiencing an encounter will move to the third stage, *Immersion/Emersion*. At this point in a Black American's Black identity development, they choose to immerse themselves in the world and culture of Black people. This is a very sensitive point in our lives because this stage can go one of three ways. The first is *disappointment and ejection*—in experiencing high levels of hopelessness we may regress back into preencounter because we do not feel there is any hope of changing the current situation. In light of this, we may instead choose to assimilate, as best we can, back to the societal norm. The second is *continuation and fixation*, where we remain stuck in the third stage, experiencing traumatic frustration and anger with the world and our place in it. The third option is the transition into the fourth stage of Black identity development, *Internalization/Commitment.* Here we as Black people develop internal security about our race and become receptive to hearing plans of change for the racial climate in the country. Additionally, secure in our own definition of Blackness, we are willing to mobilize and speak up for change for not only ourselves but also for others.

"Ohhh Child, Things are Going to Get Easier": Well-Being through Resilience

During a time when achieving a complete state of well-being or positive internalized identity, by definition, would be difficult for anybody, it is even more important that we be mindful not to embrace our Western urge to understand these stages in a rigid form. What I mean by this is that it is not helpful to think that Black people move through Black identity from stages 1 to stage 4 in chronological order and, then, once having arrived at stage 4, never leave. Black people's experience of their identity within an oppressive environment can be quite fluid. To use myself as an example, it was hard for me at times to believe there would be any significant change in the world regarding racial justice, as I heard everyday people begin to accept even more absurd excuses from leaders for blatant forms of racism. This often left me feeling dejected and wanting to just give up working toward liberation.

So, as we return to a state of *normalcy,* we need to ask ourselves what exactly that means. Normalcy would imply a return to a holistic state of health for all people; however, I don't believe this would include Black men. Because of the continued history of social injustice through generations, after the conclusion of the COVID-19 pandemic, Black men will only return to their previous state of resilience required to contend with the pandemic of racial injustice.

4

Laying Foundations

Soon I will be doing my best to walk you through the individual stories and collective themes from six Black men across the country that I interviewed. However, it is my belief that I need to be mindful of a broad dynamic taking place in our Country regarding the validity of sources of information. I recognize that I am writing this at a time in which many people have shared studies that were poorly created or, sadly, create blatant fallacies that are intended to produce realities that do not exist. I originally wrote this chapter to thoroughly articulate the theoretical foundation for the methodology I selected including research development/design, participant selection, interviews, assimilation/analysis of data, and researcher considerations, specifically the principal researcher, myself, and the audit team's background and position related to the present topic. In short, I want to demonstrate that what I did was credible and accurate. At the same time, I want to ensure that this section and everything that follows is still easily accessible for those people who are not researchers, but want to be able to have a general idea of what I did to engage in everyday conversations with people in their life. As a result, this chapter is a brief description of my research approach. If you would like to read the entirety of my methods, I have included them at the end of the book.

Theories

I used narrative analysis to capture, as best I could, the stories of social injustice, resilience, and well-being in Black men who lived in the United States during the *twin pandemic*: the global COVID-19 pandemic and the pandemic of injustices against them and their same-race peers. Additionally, I reflected on their stories by connecting them to critical race theory (CRT) in an effort to create further clarity and understanding for future research.

Narrative Analysis

I used narrative analysis because it encourages action, group mobilization, and sense of belonging (Riessman, 2008). People are storytellers (Frank, 2010), and narrative analysis helped me create a healthy collection of lived experiences set in their cultural context (Bloomberg & Volpe, 2019). It was important to me to show you the stories of those I interviewed instead of how society reflects their narratives to the world. With the United States' history of creating and reflecting deleterious narratives of Black Americans, it is especially important to keep the power in the hands of the storytellers.

Critical Race Theory

Including CRT as a paradigm was intentional. By this point, you may have read headlines such as "so and so debunks CRT" or heard battle cries from people in a state of moral panic because they heard a news anchors or politician mention that young kids were being taught to be racist by learning CRT. Of course, this isn't true. Here we will demystify CRT by talking about it. Born out of court cases such as *Brown v. Board of Education of Topeka* and established during racially charged moments like the civil rights movement of the 1960s (Delgado & Stefancic, 2017; Tate IV, 1997), CRT looks critically at social, legal, and economic systems through its five tenets: (1) racism as ordinary and not aberrational, (2) interest convergence, (3) race as a social construct, (4) storytelling and counter storytelling, and (5) structural determinism.

The first tenet simply tells us that racism exists in the United States, and it is not rare. It wants for us to unpack how America largely pushes a narrative of meritocracy and color blindness on the surface, while at a deeper level it actively marginalizes Black people by denying its responsibility for the strife they face, all in an effort to maintain the systemic power of *Whiteness* in society. This process leads to many White people believing their success is entirely due to hard work and merit without the advantages of racial privilege. In our country all White people, without choice, benefit from the color of their skin.

The second tenet, interest convergence, refers to the way that White people who hold positions of power support racial justice only insofar as it benefits them and no further, and often at the expense of Black people. This tenet helps us understand that their actions are not born of virtue, or a desire to right wrongs, but financial or public relational gains. While examples of this are innumerable, an often overlooked one is the pillage of the Negro Leagues' talent by Major League Baseball (MLB) (Rhoden, 2006). If you received similar schooling to mine, we crammed all our conversations about Black people to February. Every year, one of those lessons was the story of Jackie Robinson's integration of baseball, told to us as a clear and pure triumph for social justice issues and societal progress in America. However, it was not until later in my educational life that I learned about the role of systemic oppression in his story.

The Negro Leagues became increasingly successful before and extending after the Great Depression. Their market share increased, and people of all races frequented the games, watching talent that without question displayed more swagger and, some would argue, was better than that in the MLB. Negro Leagues owner Rube Foster knew this and was the first to make a move. He attempted to collaborate with the MLB by merging the Negro League teams into the MLB. His idea would keep the teams together, and it would also mean that Black owners would still have a seat at the table. Courtesy of their own racism, the MLB found itself caught between a rock and a hard place: allow Black players and owners into your league, or continue to bleed money.

MLB owners knew it would be in their best interest to use the Negro League players for their own profit while refusing give the players power. Led by Branch Rickey, White owners took advantage of the sociopolitical climate in at the time, targeting Black communities' psychological and real-life marginalization. They created tantalizing offers for Black Negro League players to play in the MLB, marketing it as an opportunity to "mainstream" the players and their communities. However, the pillaging of the Negro League's talent proved to be the end of the Negro League era. The owners were not integrated into the MLB, and in many cases they received no compensation for the players that were taken. After his baseball career, Jackie Robinson refused to participate in MLB events because they continued to block Black leadership (Dreier, 2013). And so we can see, by using interest convergence, how the White owners of the MLB used their power to maintain their privilege.

The third tenet of CRT, race as a social construct, refers specifically to the social construction of race for the benefit of White people. If you're unfamiliar with this, I recommend you begin by looking up examples such as the "one drop rule" that attempted to defend White people's belief in their own purity—and subsequent privileges—by stating that any drop of Black blood means you are Black (Khanna, 2010)[3], or

Dred Scott v. Sandford (Allen, 2010) to see the effect of creating a racial hierarchy for the benefit of White Americans to the detriment of Black Americans. Whether by personality or intelligence, there stands no genetic difference between races (Delgado & Stefancic, 2017). However, through *differential racialization* social scales are taught by a dominant group (i.e., White people) who create racial categories and assign positive and negative meaning to each. You may recall Linnaeus's description of Black people as "phlegmatic, cunning, lazy, lustful, careless and governed by caprice" (Degruy, 2017, p. 43) from chapter 1. In contrast, he defined his fellow White Europeans as "fickle, sanguine, blue eyed, gentle and governed by laws." Notice a difference? Definitions such as this, considered scientific, paved the way for an obsession on white beauty and superiority. Enter stage right, Johann Friedrich Blumenbach, a *scientist* who capitalized on the foundation set by Linneaus. In his book *Outcast from Evolution*, John Haller describes how Blumenbach considered visible appearances to create his classification, and to this day we continue to use a term he created, Caucasian. This name that we often use to refer to White people—ironically thinking it's more socially acceptable than calling someone White—Blumenbach took from the Caucasus mountains, which, according to biblical scripture, are where Noah's ark landed. In all his scientific

---

[3] See Dr. Yaba Blay's book *One Drop* for more information.

methodology, he believed this location to be the origin of "the most beautiful race" and thus adequate for the "original race of man," White people. From then to now, societal dynamics continue to create and continue miseducation on racial differences.

Sue et al. (2019, p. 259) points to CRT's fourth tenet, storytelling and counter storytelling, by asking the rhetorical question, "If you want to understand oppression, should you ask the oppressor or the oppressed?" Counter storytelling is largely based on the powerful tool of slave narratives, which gave necessary voice to the oppression endured by slaves and dissented from the societal narrative of slavery as a "good thing." Counter storytelling continues to be essential today because we know that the mainstream stories often told in schools and politics are often biased (Hackman & Rauscher, 2004). It is imperative to have counter storytelling to ensure that the stories of those oppressed are being voiced.

The fifth tenet of CRT, structural determinism, is "the view that there are structural elements or factors that deterministically affect outcomes, events, or processes" (Clegg & Bailey, 2008). In the context of our conversation, this means that our systems function in a way that centralizes and prioritizes whiteness and white culture while degrading blackness and black culture. As a result, we are determined to repeat the same cycle until we readjust the structures at their core. One example of this is language. In our country we both lack the necessary language to better explain and deal with racism in our systems, and use language that actively or passively defends this harmful dynamic. Specifically, we can look at the language we use in our laws, policies, and everyday life that protects whiteness. A recent example of this is Governor Ron DeSantis's "Stop W.O.K.E Act," which put strict limitations on potential DEI discussion within the state of Florida. According to an Associated Press report, this act in practice blocked a school in his state from teaching an AP (advanced placement) African American studies course. With language such as this that defends racism and without the language to describe racism, racist actions will continue to develop variations in all societal systems, with subsequently no way to rectify them (Delgado & Steffancic, 2016).

Statement of the Problem

With the first global health pandemic in over a century, the world experienced unique problems that were new to our generation and that disproportionately impacted marginalized communities, including Black men. While the COVID-19 health pandemic was happening, experiences of social injustice did not cease for Black men in the United States. This created a novel experience where in the midst of the health pandemic, Black men simultaneously needed reservoirs of resilience for their own well-being as they continued to be recipients of and witnesses to inequality.

As previously stated, resilience as a response to trauma can be normal and necessary to maintain one's sense of self and one's well-being (Tedeschi & Calhoun, 2004). However, many of the stories told regarding Black experiences include only the barriers and obstacles they face, such as increases in discrimination (Ruiz et al., 2020), while additionally only showing people's pain and struggle. While it is important to explicate the atrocities that have and continue to be directed toward Black people, to truly grasp the experience we must also highlight within these stories Black resilience, perseverance, and joy through these struggles.

In my research exploration, no study to date had taken a narrative approach to telling the stories of Black men in the pandemic that included resilience and well-being while using CRT to root their experience in a connected history. I was my intention to bring to light the unique phenomenology present in our experiences. I ask that you take your time reading through these stories by putting the book down between chapters and reflecting on your experience of what you read and how it applies to your life. This brings us to our conversations . . .

Introduction to Results

> You see you wouldn't ask why the rose that grew from the concrete had damaged petals. On the contrary, we would all celebrate its tenacity. We would all love its will to reach the sun. Well, we are the rose—this is the concrete—and these are my damaged petals. Don't ask me why, thank God, ask me how!
>
> (Tupac Shakur, 1989)

The purpose of this study was to gain a better understanding of what the past few years have been like for Black men surviving the twin-pandemic: social injustice and COVID-19. To do this, I interviewed six Black men from different geographical locations within the United States (Table 1). I focused on four major questions: First, how did Black men show resilience through the past year in regard to managing the twin-pandemic? Second, in what ways did Black men experience their well-being during the twin pandemic? Third, in what ways did participants' interpersonal relationships with family, friends, and community play a role in their own resilience and well-being and the resilience and well-being of others? And, fourth, did participants show resilience strategies they had learned from previous generations or from their community (such as parents, grandparents, and mentors) in handling their problems during the twin-pandemic? Each participant has a pseudonym. I intentionally selected each of their names based on the strengths they showed not only in our interview but in their life. "Matt" represents me as the interviewer.

Table 1

The Roses

Participant	Age	Race/ Ethnicity	Sexual Orient.	Career	SES	Parent	State
Izaak (Laughter)	28	Black	Queer	Telecom sales	Middle	No	PA
Oscar (God's spear)	60	Black	Het.	Student/ Teacher	Middle	Yes	TX/ KS
Niles (Champion)	52	Black	Het.	Self-employed CEO	Middle	Yes	MD
Zahair (Shining bright)	28	Black American	Het.	Analyst	Undis-closed	No	GA
Marcel (Young warrior)	26	African American	Het.	School Supervisor	Middle	No	CA
Atukwei (Intuitive, Creative)	31	Black/ Ghanaian	Het.	HR	Middle	No	CO

The participants' experiences allowed for themes and subthemes to emerge from the four major questions. It is important to note that while the themes and subthemes created from the interviews are discussed in this section individually, their relationship with each other, meaning the participants' experiences, have a much more interwoven dynamic that influences their holistic experience and responses to adversity. In sum, the chapters that follow are intended to provide a detailed story, which considers specific context of these men, their respective systems, and how they relate to each other (Bloomberg & Volpe, 2019).

Major Questions, Themes, and Subthemes

1. How did Black men show resilience through the past year in regard to managing the twin-pandemics of COVID-19 and social injustice?
    a. Superpowers

2. In what ways did Black men experience their well-being during the twin pandemic?
    a. Experiences of Racism/prejudice (Expect them)
    b. Creative coping strategies for well-being
        i. Close your circle
        ii. Physical/mental health
        iii. Strong Black identity

3. In what ways did participants' interpersonal relationships with family, friends, and community play a role in their own resilience and well-being and the resilience and well-being of others?
    a. Same-race peer support/scrutiny
    b. Experiences of white peer interactions

        i. White accountability / recognition
        ii. White lack of awareness = distancing
    c. Generalized social experiences
        i. Silver linings
        ii. Inspiring the next generation

4. Did participants show resilience strategies learned from previous generations or their community (such as mothers, fathers, and grandparents) in handling their problems over the last year?
    a. Learning from past or previous generations

5

Superpowers

Do not get lost in a sea of despair.
Be hopeful, be optimistic.
Our struggle is not the struggle of a day, a week, a month, or a year,
it is the struggle of a lifetime.
Never, ever be afraid to make some noise and get in good trouble,
necessary trouble.
(John Lewis, 1963)

Enter static: The focused build-up to a futuristic sound protected and owned by a knocking percussion. My head felt it, the iconic beat of The Weeknd's "Pray for Me," made famous in the 2018 movie, *Black Panther*. Mid-interview, in every interview, I could see clear the superhuman skills these men had and the feats they were able to accomplish as a result. Inspired by compassion and in search of peace, there was a poised ferocity that filled the room each time. They were, in Abel's words, "always ready for a war again." For the challenge of being a Black man in America, all six of the Black men I spoke to indirectly described using *abilities* that allowed them to traverse the last few years during the twin-pandemic. Their responses to adversity felt so powerful to me as the interviewer that I thought it best to call them superpowers.

Adaptability

One of the men, Izaak, described being a chameleon able to adapt to any situation: "You gotta kinda be fluid or be able to adapt and almost be chameleon-like. And I think that's just a lot of my day-to-day when it comes to being Black in America." An already existing fluidity to adapt to circumstances made tasks that many people had difficulty with, such as adjusting to working from home, easy for him: "They gave us like a Lowe's box, like you got fired, and said, 'Take it home, we'll figure it out from there.' So (laughs) . . . I kind of like made it work." When I asked how he made the transition appear seamless, he mentioned an acceptance: "At the end of the day the sun still going to shine in the morning. You know, days are going to go on, time's going to keep flying."

To be a chameleon the men had to learn the colors of their ever-changing environments. For Atukwei, this meant at times having to play into oppressive systems to maintain his safety:

> Knowing exactly what the stereotypes [are], knowing that, okay, if I get pulled over, they're

> already thinking these things. So what do I have to do to make sure that these officers aren't thinking these things. And that's an act of colluding with oppression. The fact that we have to think about, oh shit how am I going to survive? How am I going to do this? How am I going to get out of this situation alive? We have to collude with oppression to survive and get out of that space. And so like I learned that shit when I was in middle school, high school.

Izaak found himself colluding with oppression in his life as well. He told me how he responded when riots burst out after National Guard troops were sent to occupy his city: "Don't leave the house. Don't leave to get the food . . . like you gotta hear your mother say . . . They're robbin' so-and-so on 5th street, they're car-jacking in the neighborhood . . . Be careful out there."

The chameleon ability allowed these Black men to constantly be aware of their environment, including being mindful of the types of people they spent time around and cues about who to avoid such as, "the people that say, 'I don't see color," (Izaak). Or "someone who was saying something like a blue lives matter . . . I may have already put them in a category of people like racists or, like, I don't wanna fuck with them," which he noted was because "[I] don't feel safe." For the majority of Black men I spoke to, it was a lack of awareness among White people that made them create distance from them.

Communication and Critical Thinking

Despite being on the front lines of adversity, these men used their flexible thinking to learn from other's opinions through literature or direct communication about COVID-19 and social movements such as BLM protests. As Izaak explains: "A lot of those conversations for me are very informative on my part . . . me learning about the situation, understanding that . . . it's kind of an embedded thing in the system."

Moreover, Zahair showed his power of connecting with others in a place of not knowing, "I believe in order to get someone else to see your viewpoint, you have to talk to everybody, [including] people that you disagree with." One way he engaged in this was by speaking to people from different political parties, "I've talked to Democrats, [I've talked] to Republicans. I've talked to Independents." And by inviting critical dialogue around current events, such as George Floyd's murder, he was able to find common ground with many people, "I've asked them, you know, what do they think about it? . . . [and there was] consensus [in] most of them. They're like, yeah, I just can't like, I just can't justify it."

Others married critical thinking, learned information, and tested heuristics to navigate and survive. Oscar, for instance, noticed low vaccination rates in the Black community: "Brothers wasn't getting shots. . . . And they were all going back to what, to Tuskegee." As a PhD student, he tried to extend his knowledge to help others, "I said look man, hold up, hold up this is different because they [gave] White people the same thing right . . . (laughs)." He additionally used this approach in comprehending the murder of Ahmaud Arbery: "He's running, minding his business. And they take it upon themselves, right? Cause you know how White people like to do, they like to control Black, Black male bodies." Likewise, he identified the differential treatment of BIPOC individuals or groups in comparison to the January 6th insurrectionists, "In the seventies . . . some Puerto Rican nationalists . . . went into the Congress. Just like those guys did. They got twenty-five years. Twenty-five years![4] Now I'm seeing these people get forty months, six months. I'm like really that's not, that's not, that's not right."

Oscar is all too aware of the "cudgel" used to perpetuate systemic White supremacy, and he used his knowledge to undo the miseducation implicit in our systems. I felt like I was listening to a structured analysis as I heard him articulate a powerful experience of unchecked White supremacy palpable during this twin-pandemic:

> I've noticed something about White people. That they think that stuff belongs to them. That all

[4] Shooting at the U.S. Capitol in 1954; see Shapiro 2021.

> the hard work has only been done by White people. Everything that they've earned they earn it legitimately, right. What they don't realize is that they're standing on third base, thinking they hit a triple, when really they're the pinch runner. . . . I'm a historian also, right. So I know all the work that was done by slaves. [Matt: Yeah.] I know all the work that was done by the Chinese Americans . . . where they built, helped build a railroad. I know about the Mexicans who came from Mexico and worked in the lands, right. I know about all this stuff. So I know what minorities have done for this country. But we haven't been privy to all the advantages of being White, you know.

Moreover, he used connections from the histories of injustice, including from his own family history of sharecropping, "My great grandfather was alive during Reconstruction. So to know that Black people, especially Black men, are still being treated as lesser than kind of hit home." The mental process he goes through to understand current events also extended into conversation about George Floyd's murder and the "shock" he had witnessing "a White guy [who] had his knee on the . . . back of a Black man's neck." He immediately tied this to a description of Black men as "endangered species . . . [who] die from, you know, drugs or police or whatever, you know."[5]

Alchemy

In addition to these powers were the Alchemists. One definition of an alchemist is someone who transforms things for the better. It may appear in some instances that these individuals are creating something from nothing; however, this is far from the case. Their experience, sadly, is one that is far too human and shared among Black men. The humanity of these people is no more or less than anyone. At the same time, they take what some consider the heaviest of life's burdens as materials to be transformed for the betterment of all. For Niles, it begins with trudging through his own pains,

> You know, through this time Matt . . . it's been like kind of rock bottom for me. [Matt: Yeah.] [You] know, I lost twenty-five or more people to COVID, [Matt: Damn.] Several other family members I lost. Maybe ten or fifteen of my young people to murder. I've lost three of my best friends that I grew up with me to violent murder. My mom is in ICU fighting for her life. [Matt: Yeah.] Fighting for her life for two years.

He then converted his grief into compassionate community change for Black residents, "I'm always big on

[5] Here he is referring to the concept of Black male exceptionalism; see Guy 2014.

what's the change, you know, what can we do to be better? What's the solution? . . . I'm, let's roll our sleeves up and get on this whiteboard. And let's put a plan together and let's go execute." It is his powerful empathy that drives him to create. His resolve is connected to his upbringing in the hoods of Maryland, which required resilience to survive. During the twin-pandemic, he sees in people an all-too-familiar fear of unexpected death that once weighed on him and members of his community at young ages, "It used to be a time when you grew up in a hood. You will say, man, I'm not going live past eighteen or I'm not gone live past twenty-two or I don't have nothing to live for." Although he has seen Black people making strides, during the twin-pandemic he feared that COVID-19 and oppressive political policy/rhetoric would take away the gains in independence Black people have made. He explained, "People are very facetious, and they calculated in their way of making sure [Black] life dissipates. So we gotta, we gotta pay attention. Because that's what the, the, the, the Trump administration was about. That's why they needed that, another four." For Niles, this is why he must use his superpower, not only in the sociopolitical sector but the policing sector as well, where he finds his current plans entrenched in social change between his community and police departments, "We got to teach people. So we're going to teach the police officers how to deal with citizens. [Matt: Yeah.] . . . just because you're a police officer, don't mean you know how to deal with people."

Racism within the United States is a sad inevitability, as Niles says: "Yes, it's social injustice. No, I don't agree with the system, but we already knew that." As a result, creating something from negative circumstances was necessary. When met with this adversity, Marcel created motivation from his rage: "You kinda wanna prove them wrong. . . . Yeah, they do see me as evil and . . . [at the same time] I'm as high as I can get [in my career]. So [now] I have a lot of respect from a lot of people who I either didn't have it from at first, or didn't want to give it to me at first." He continued explaining how he morphed their assumptions into motivation, "It eats at you, you know, or it feeds you, gives you motivation. . . . I'm not just another statistic."

For Oscar, however, it meant turning his rage toward racism in education, by educating the masses through research, as well as teaching teachers, "I want people to know in education that you can't, you can't keep treating Black kids like this." The system has created a fire within many Black men that burns bright, and for Oscar it is his current catalyst for change within the mostly White teacher subsystem he is surrounded by, "I get fired up right. And I get fired up because I teach teachers right, and you know all these teachers. . . . They're shocked. Shocked. Just shocked. I said, I don't know why you're being shocked. . . . This is what's been going on for years."

***

I felt humbled by just how much effort and resilience these men displayed. Yet, I was far from surprised because I know there is little time for stagnation when you are a Black man. Izaak noted this as well: "I always say, you know, you have fifteen minutes to kind of bitch, moan, and complain, right. But after that fifteen minutes . . . how do we keep moving forward?" So for those engaged in alchemy, any emotion or experience only provides material to be used for creation. Niles puts it this way: "I make sure I stay the course on my projects . . . [so they] can create change that can help us have a seat at the table and a voice. And [then we'll] have an even playing field with the social injustice."

One of the things I greatly appreciated about all the people I spoke to was the diversity in their approaches for interacting with the world. For Zahair, to find a place of positive well-being he needed to remove himself from the sidelines and take action. Upon finding out that nothing was going to happen with the murder of Breonna Taylor, he leveraged his emotional pain and rage to make a difference for peace and equity. However, as someone who is immune-compromised due to a heart condition, he found himself hesitating, balancing the serious risk to his health with his desire to do more to fight injustice. Regardless, after consultation and preparation he led a march to the belly of the beast, "I kinda just bit the bullet and actually led a March in [city name], a protest . . . to this store called Wildman's, it's a racist store . . . they sell KKK clothes and like nooses and things like that." His spur the moment march expected 50 people, but it became something greater, with approximately two thousand in attendance and a police escort. Though this action is traditionally outside of his personality, he chose to use his ability to become a pillar for change.

Connected to these superpowers was a strong understanding of their own Black identities, with many rooted in a belief that they can and must overcome. For instance, Izaak told me: "You can't rely on other people, or I don't expect to. I don't expect anything or anyone." Whether for himself or his family, Izaak felt as though he had to always be ready to be a rock during the twin-pandemic, "To me. It's like . . . making sure everyone around me is good. So I want to focus on like my mom who's got her [multiple sclerosis]. And her ailments, my brother, anything that he needs."

Additionally, a positive Black identity often looked like standing up for Black life; however, in order to do this Oscar sometimes needed to accept being branded as a hater of White people. Regardless, Oscar remained unstirred, even when confronted with America's racial miseducation in his own home, when his daughter asked if he hated White people after she noticed he was calling them out for discriminatory and prejudicial behavior. His response, however, gave me joy: "I said, no, I don't hate White people. I just love Black people." For those naive to the causes of racial justice, we are very much living in a time in which a person's love of Black people presumes hating White people. But Oscar's knowledge of the world and our past prepared him for any adversity, and he does not shy away from it, "Don't come up [with] no nonsense around me because I'mma blast you and I'm not toning it down." Moreover, with the privilege of his education he shares his knowledge on difficult topics such as CRT through writing, in hopes we all grow, "I wrote an op-ed. . . . I said yeah you need to teach CRT, but this is called culturally relevant teaching. You need to teach that . . . you need to know about what the impact that Black people [have] made in this country."

Born in Ghana but raised in the United States since 2000, Atukwei had to learn what it meant to have Black skin while living in America, "My whole world [was] learning [what] it means to be an African in America." Because his parents were from Ghana, his lessons about racism had to come firsthand without the beneficial reconnaissance of stories from previous generations,

> I was experiencing racism in middle school, but obviously I didn't know what it was. . . . I remember the first time when I got pulled over and my friend, my two African friends who were with me, we just we left a soccer practice and they see us three, the cops see us three leave the soccer practice and we're like, why the fuck you pulling us over? You literally, we just left practice, we saw you and

> we got pulled over, we got strip searched like everybody driving looking at us and I went home, and I couldn't talk to my parents about it.

Atukwei needed to take initiative to figure out what was going on by himself, "I didn't learn that from my parents. We didn't have any conversations about the Black Code you know . . . and I was like, shit, this would of been nice for my parents to talk to me about."

While these Black men were able to use their superpowers to survive or succeed, there were also side effects of overusing them. For example, Marcel talked about his experience growing up as a Black man, "[We're] taught that like our feelings and emotions and stuff like that don't matter. . . . So I just used like . . . socioeconomic status and . . . financial status . . . factors [to] like push me instead, right." Compartmentalization can be an adaptive strategy, but overuse has side effects, as Marcel explained, "[I] completely like wrote off, my mental and emotional . . . not realizing like, you know, like the core of me is entirely depleting." Oscar was also aware of the side effects of overusing his skills: "I think I got too intellectual. . . . I think I lost myself as a person because I was just thinking about all the things that I study." Using his superpower was helpful and often necessary; at the same time he noted how he was unable to find his humanity until the harsh denial of another's was forced on him when he saw George Floyd's video, "He's a grown man, he's got he's got a mom. . . . He's got family members who care and love him. . . . He's got a daughter who cares, loves him." It was reflection on this experience that brought him back, "Finally, I finally snapped out that, you know."

Interpretations and Synthesis

Human beings are wildly adaptable to adversity (Ungar, 2011), and as a therapist I try my best to walk alongside my clients as they reclaim their power by reconstructing harmful narratives about aspects of themselves, that were created by systems and people (White & Epston, 1990). Engaging in this reclamation some such as myself, refer to it as superpowers. The phraseology I used is not unique to the Black men I interviewed. At the same time, the consistent need to develop, use, and reuse superpowers in the face of extraordinary adversity was unique to their experiences. As I tried my best to put myself in their shoes, each time the fit was familiar: a need to constantly be "super." While adversity is inevitable in human life, the comments and stories of these Black men suggest that they experienced common adversities shared among most people due to COVID-19, such as having to adjust to working from home (Sunday et al., 2021; Xiao et al., 2021;) and increases in negative emotional experiences such as anxiety, depression and, isolation (Liu et al., 2020; AlHumaid et al., 2020). In addition, however, they faced adversities unique to their experience as Black men. This included, but was not limited to fearing they could lose their life from not just COVID-19, but living in systemically underresourced areas that create higher crime and higher infection, police violence, and civilian violence. They also faced rhetoric from the former president, the media, and everyday people denying historic and present racism.

Moreover, I observed a surrounding experience of oppression from our already discriminatory health care, policing, and legal systems also played out in public. All of these required additional resilience in order to maintain well-being and safety.

As humans, we possess the creative ability to employ a variety of tactics to solve our problems (Aldous, 2005; Isaksen et al., 2011), and the powers mentioned before—blending in as a chameleon, intellectually inspired heuristics, alchemy, and creating community—are examples of this. Further, they made it clear to me that superpowers can come in bunches and look different for each individual. It was remarkable how these men showed their ability to switch between or use multiple powers if necessary. For example, Izaak leaned heavily on being a chameleon to survive interactions with individuals who held negative beliefs about Black people. But he also showed his historical knowledge to create heuristics about his present environment for his well-being. Further, none of these men stopped at their own well-being. In fact, the majority described efforts to undo their painful experiences by dismantling oppressive systems through various means such as reform in schools, police trainings, community events, and music. While they may have wished, as Zahair did, to "just . . . wake up, eat a bagel, go to work . . . workout after work. . . . eat a steak or something and just like go to sleep," they recognized an inescapable need to be super in their everyday lives, for themselves and others.

Lastly, participants' ability to survive during this time by using their powers was remarkable. At the same time, many mentioned negative side effects of overuse that impacted their well-being. For example, prolonged intellectualization in order to survive the twin-pandemic was felt as a double-edged sword. While it was needed, and helped them throughout this time, the cost was experienced as a loss of humanity. Others found themselves adjacent to hopelessness after depleting their energy to resist destructive narratives, oppressive systems, and apathetic people. This connects to existing literature that tells us prolonged resilience usually has negative effects on mental health (Brooks et al., 2020; Liu et al., 2012).

Contemporary research has examined the effects of being in a state of resilience during COVID-19 and found mixed results (Kira, 2022; Manchia, 2022). In many cases the studies found that people were successfully managing the COVID-19 pandemic by being resilient, despite the toll it was taking on mental health. However, my study specifically looked at Black men and included the impact of social injustice; it found having to be in a constant state of resilience had detrimental effects for Black men.

To explain this discrepancy, let me return to the benefit of CRT's structural determinism. While I was trying to understand my experience and the experiences of people who hold skin color similar to mine, I found that many studies, both during the twin-pandemic and prior to it, did not include contextual components such as social injustice in the creation of their models of psychological distress. The overwhelming majority, in fact, neglected to see the fraternal twin of injustice that was born into America before COVID-19 and, more specifically, failed to see how the inequitable and discriminatory responses to COVID-19 by race were predictable based on prior injustices. This has left gaps in our understanding of racial discrimination that then shows up in news articles and television programs, leading to even greater misunderstanding by our fellow countrymen and women. In essence, the lack of understanding perpetuates an incorrect narrative about racial progress and a lack of sufficient reflective research on marginalized experiences.

6

Experiences of Racism and Prejudice (expect them)

Two words, United States, no love, no breaks
Low brow, high stakes . . . everybody move.
(Yasiin Bey, 2004)

Speaking to these Black men about experiences of racism was one of the most difficult parts of writing this for you. In part, because of the emotional toll it took on me, but honestly it was more the pressure I placed on myself to do justice to their experiences. And, frankly, their experiences were so wide and diverse, it felt impossible to create a linear narrative of the short common approach to literary writing in the West. Maybe it's the fiery words of Yasiin Bey playing in my Beats that inspired my moment of dissident enlightenment: I did not have to fit this mold that was a product of my White-centric education. So my hope is that you allow yourself to experience the unpredictable crash of different racially charged experiences and responses, which, depending on your identities, may feel familiar or foreign to you. Regardless, know that the only common thread in these men's stories was that no one was surprised.

The societal archetype of Black male inferiority we discussed in previous chapters was thoroughly felt in the Black community during this time, especially in response to large social movements. For example, Izaak described opponents to Black Lives Matter as not seeing the "reality" of the message, "I don't think the intent [of BLM] was, you know, like [Black people as] a superior race kind of thing . . . the bottom line was they matter. . . . I just feel like the bar was low. The word 'matter' was the bar." In comparison, acts of White privilege were quickly seen and felt. For example, when asked about the experience of seeing the January 6 insurrections, Izaak talked about conversations he had with same-race peers,

> You can see a mob of White folks that are literally mobbing and climbing and breaking windows and busting down, being violent. And it feels like . . . they kinda let it happen. [And] a lot my Black friends [would] say like, let that be Black people . . . the entire National Guard would have been there on site. Guns drawn. There had been lives. There would've been lives . . . only they could, they being White people, can get away with something as vile or something as wild as that, but

> let the same scenario just flip the race of the person that's there. You can see it being a way more dangerous or a way more violent situation.

Meanwhile all Black men I spoke to found their lives heavily restricted during this time, as Izaak notes: "I remember at one point, [the] National Guard were driving around the city and I was scared to go downtown just so I don't get mistaken for somebody, you know what I mean?" Additionally, five of six men talked to me about expending cognitive energy on "what if" scenarios regarding police interactions grounded in family and historical stories about differential treatment of Black people by police. Izaak explained, "There's always been a distrust with the police. So [it's] even more now. . . . I was always taught turn a light on or put a light on, hands where you can see them kind of thing, just so there's no confusion . . . not giving them the opportunity to see what happens."

Regardless of the officer(s) intentions, police interactions, or the fear of impending police interactions, had powerful negative impacts on psychological and physiological functioning, such as surges of anxiety and heart palpitations that required grounding techniques and active problem solving. Marcel explained what it is like for him:

> I don't feel comfortable ever when a police officer gets behind me. . . . I'll get in borderline like

hyperventilation, like my heart fluttering. And I'm like constantly checking. And I'll have to do self-checks, like dude you have your license, you have your registration . . . there's no warrant for your arrest. I gotta tell myself, these things [to] come to earth . . . realizing now [it's] like, no, you're not worried about any of those things, you're worried about how are you going to treated when you're pulled over by this person, right. Or you're worried about what this person looks like when you get pulled over. [Hoping] they're going to be some kind of like Latin or, God, please like African American. And if not like, how is this interaction gonna go like that's what, that's what you're feeling this why you're feeling this way because all the shit you see on the news, right. And all these lives that are being taken away, right. . . . And you do all the little weird things like [if a] cop is coming behind [me] . . . I'm making like two right turns park in a gas station, I don't even need gas, right. But I'm just avoiding any interaction at all costs. And realizing like, like why the fuck am I doing [that] . . . bro like I fuckin damn near have a panic attack it's insane. . . . It's the saddest honestly, but the scariest and the most real thing that I do now is like I keep my wallet and all that immediately like in my cup holder, right there, it's cause I hear all

> the stories about like people going to reach for their wallet in their back pocket. Or they go to reach for the glove compartment, [and] people are like trigger-happy. . . . So now my, my wallet's right there, like is it okay if I grab it? It's like why the fuck do I need permission? Like that's just the thing that I feel like I've grown accustomed to doing as a survival tactic, which it's sad, man, sad.

I asked Oscar, as a military veteran, to share his experience of public scrutiny for our policing and military systems. He noted that racist beliefs once had to be covert, "If you were racist in the military, that would be the end of your career." However, he shared that he feels as though racism found safe haven during the Trump administration, "Today, they [had] straight up people [with] the 'Trump train,' wearing their Trump hats." This impacts his state of mind: "If I see any Trump supporter automatically, I think racist. . . . If you, if you adhere to him to what he says, you support him, he's a racist." While he recognizes that many people in the military are not racist and are bothered by support for racist policies and action, seeing Trump merchandise on his military base enraged him and caused him to create distance, "I go on base I see people with Trump [stuff], I'm like damn! . . they're not trying to hide it . . . He made it okay to hate."

Continuing in the area of policing in the United States, participants Izaak, Oscar, Zahair, and Atukwei again stated a difference in how the police treated BLM protesters and January 6 insurrectionists, showing me that this was an exceptionally difficult experience. Oscar, for instance, said: "If that had been five brothers, they'd have been dead." For Zahair, conversations with others around January 6 were the most difficult. Specifically noting how protests with majority Black people or with the goals of protecting Black life led to arrests, even when the protests had permits, he told me, "We were doing a protest every single day . . . walking from parks, walking from the city in the middle of the street, like everything you know. . . . And then to see people actually raid the Capitol. . . . Like the Capitol? Like the Capitol, like you're just gonna, the Capitol?" He experienced pain from the juxtaposition of insurrectionists' joyful expressions of triumph for "domestic terrorism" with his personal experiences of being punished for using his rights under the First Amendment. He said, "For us not be able to do that was kind of disheartening because like, [does] the First Amendment no[t] apply to Black people?" Additionally, Zahair, like others, shared his anger toward former President Trump's role in what happened, "[You] had the President saying, yeah, go down there and do it. Like what, you had the president telling you to go riot?" Similar to Izaak, Zahair's well-being was negatively affected by the sociopolitical climate and the presence of National Guard troops who were deployed to his city as well, "Yeah, they came to [city's name] . . . and I was just like that can't be what I think it is. And then the next day, they were like yeah, President Trump has ordered, like, the National Guard to go to certain cities."

With decades of removing and or underfunding resources in areas that have majority Black residents and intensified policing during the twin-pandemic in these areas, participants' ability to blend into their environment could not save them from the harsh realities around them. In my conversation with Izaak it was here that I noticed a fear and exhaustion, which he then expressed, "It's like you started thinking like, you know, I don't think about dying every goddamn day you know what I mean, but . . . I think more about like my safety and well-being just by stepping out my damn door. . . . So it's that I only feel safe when I'm in my room." Despite this, he was able to illustrate his understanding of the deadly dance that systemic racism creates in majority Black communities, and he displayed empathy for those few people rioting, "When our voices aren't being heard, you'll see destruction. . . . I don't think the intent is always, let's go riot. I think it's like let's protest, but alright now, we're rioting."

When COVID-19 caused restrictions in everyday lives, people tried to come up with strategies, such as physical activity, to maintain well-being. Oscar tried make sure he got outside, "So I decided to walk around the neighborhood . . . minding my business." However, engaging in this strategy was only part of his story: "As I'm coming home, I'm walking this way. Some White women are walking that way. They damn near lost their mind. I was like, no, hell no. . . . I don't want nothing from you. there's nothing you have that I want, right." As I previously said, racism was expected; however, some of the Black men I interviewed still had a visceral experience of rage, and rightly so. Unable to undo these women's prejudices, it sadly became the work of Oscar to make the adjustment, "It did something to me. I stopped walking around the neighborhood without my wife." Despite being financially well-off from previously serving in the military, he and his wife felt like they were being treated as second-class citizens in their neighborhood. Further, he spoke to the emotions he experienced from this incident,

> It pissed me off. When I got home, I told my wife about it. I was like these two damn White girls and that's what they were. They weren't women. They were girls, young girls maybe about nineteen, twenty. And the, just the fear, I'm, I'm like, damn I live here too! This my neighborhood too. What gives you the right to think that it only belongs to you?

Since the twin-pandemic, experiences of racism felt heightened for some participants, and in some ways became more apparent, as Oscar comments: "The racism that I've seen from, from Whites it's just off the charts, man. . . . This pandemic has brough out the ugliness . . . the inequalities." Even in states such as California, which is perceived as progressive, it is far from the case, according to Marcel. With a high cost of living and low minimum wages, life during the twin-pandemic was difficult. While experiencing a health and social pandemic, California, for him, continued to centralize its wealth and resources in majority-White areas. Further, authentic attempts to make things more equitable always came up short in Marcel's eyes: "It's always like super radical movements happen that are heavy on you and emotionally draining and physically and mentally daunting, right. But then you don't ever see results." Additionally sharing his own story of protesting and petitioning as, "feeling empowered," at first, but after not seeing results, feeling as though California's approach is one of "smoke and mirrors."

Work-related requirements during the twin-pandemic had a unique effect on these Black men. Atukwei walked me through his work life as an associate housing director. He was expected to hold conversations around many of the murders committed against Black people. It was here that he first felt the effects of the twin-pandemic on his well-being. While recognizing he had a job to do, he engaged in problem-solving and leadership, but that meant putting his well-being on the back burner.

> During that time . . . we were really hit hard. . . . And I think for me it was, it was a difficult place to be in as a Black man in leadership, especially during the pandemic. And . . . the team [was] looking [at] leadership for spaces to

> conversate. And at the same time it's like, Oh shit (laughs), I'm trying to take care of myself right now. I don't wanna, I don't want to organize a space to have a conversation.

Black men who had to work in predominantly White spaces noticed their decreased well-being in the face of performative allyship and indirect discrimination by active avoidance, and some had few options to find financial stability or success without putting up with it. Marcel, the only Black person in his organization, discussed with me the "bubble effect" created by affluence that worked to shut out racial trauma and suffering:

> I remember the height of like, you know, the social injustice and the BLM movement and all that. . . . I actually live like [close to] where the riots in [city name] area were. And [the] banks and all that were getting burned down . . . and I was having to drive up to [town name], a more affluent neighborhood for work because it's where the money's at. . . . And then like drive back to reality every day was like hard for me to like grapple because where I worked at, it kind of wasn't a thing.

For Marcel, going to work was like stepping into an alternate reality that had no interest in how he was doing. As he explained, "No one checked on me." Exiting this privileged space to return to reality meant the return of a different discomfort, "They had like tanks and the taskforce out on the streets making sure you're not driving around." The pain was so intense he contemplated leaving work numerous times, "It was hard, I honestly question where I was at in life. If I was in the correct place." To combat this, he noticed his mind having to run mental gymnastics to believe his colleagues genuinely liked him, until he couldn't avoid his truth: "I like reflect back now . . . how I had to like, go the extra mile and earn their respect to be seen as equal." This was all happening as he had to manage microaggressions such as, "He's one of the good ones. Or . . . he's not like the others." These statements had negative impacts on his psychological well-being, "as a Black man [that] kind of stuff like sits and resonates."

Finding leadership positions during the twin-pandemic did not provide an umbrella for my interviewees from the downpour of discrimination taking place across America. This was especially true for Oscar, Marcel, and Atukwei, who shared a career in educational leadership and worked in predominately White institutions (PWI). Atukwei noted that "it was very challenging. And to be honest, it was the first time in my leadership career where I was like, man, I don't know if I can, wear this hat. And . . . [I've never been in] the [position] where I just feel defeated [in] everything I'm doing." Feelings of being "isolated," discouraged, or even disheartened in their colleagues and themselves were also present, as Marcel told me: "Once this started going on in the world, like that brought up those emotions for me, and things that like I subconsciously like blocked off." Marcel again referenced lies he told himself about his colleagues, "No, you knew who these people were. . . . You chose to ignore it for the better of your own mental health and your own well-being. So I chose [to] act like you know like I'm around people who genuinely do care about me." That was difficult for him, as it felt like his colleagues refused to acknowledge what was happening to Black people, "I know we see what happened last night. Like I know we see to breaking news you know. . . . So I had to sit with that."

Not only was Marcel aware of the mental health sacrifices he accrued, but while he paid a cost, his school received the benefit of his Black identity. Specifically, as his skin color was being used as a weapon to defend the very bubble of racism he was tortured in, "there's like an ongoing joke that I'm kind of like the token, like the golden like Black male in a district where it's like . . . not only do we have a person of color here, but . . . he's really damn good at his job . . . so . . . I'm kinda like flaunted about." He feels like he is routinely moved around to different schools in part to meet quotas, and that weighs on him,

> And now you're here, and it's all like, oh this is [Marcel] this is the one we were telling you

about, and he's . . . this and this and this and blah, blah, blah. And it doesn't feel very genuine." [Matt: But like you said, they're using you for the color of your skin, and meanwhile they're also like, all that shit you come from, ya we need to redirect that you can't bring that here.] Yeah. Literally like yeah, like yeah, this is what we have, but also, remember when you're here, you're not really a Black male, you're, you're a [school name] School District classified worker.

This has left him adjacent to hopelessness, questioning if he will really be able to break through the wall of racism and achieve his success, "Can I really do it. Like can I really make more of myself . . . how far can I really get? How much can I really build for my name, my family, my lineage?"

Interpretations and Synthesis

According to CRT, racism is not an aberration (Delgado & Stefancic, 2017). Talking to participants about racism and their well-being during the twin-pandemic had an inescapable matter-of-factness. No participant expressed surprise to have experienced racism during the twin-pandemic. Additionally, I resonated with how they would provide stories from their past that helped put their current experience into context. This provided what felt like a shared understanding regarding how we had to interact with our present environment, letting me know that they, like me, had experienced the social injustice pandemic before, and most likely expected to continue experiencing injustice after COVID-19 is no longer considered a pandemic.

It is important to note that while racism was expected, it still had an impact on participants, who noted powerful negative effects on their physical health (sometimes experiencing surges of anxiety), psychological health (such as excessive cognitive energy spent trying to understand if an environment is safe), and interpersonal relationships (discussed in following themes). However, these adult Black men already knew this was the world they lived in, and they understood that further rumination or denial would only increase an already heavy burden. This is in line with previous research that talks about the need for Black families and their kids to discuss and navigate racial oppression, often at early stages in the life cycle (Hardy & Laszloffy, 2000).

It was clear that experiences of racism, from everyday microaggressions to systemic injustice, were already a part of how participants had to manage their well-being. However, with COVID-19 slowing the world down and media picking up stories of injustice, their lived experiences were much more overtly talked about. This allowed for an opportunity of scrutiny or acceptance. It is perhaps possible that the unpredictable nature of conversations about race—essentially not knowing how someone will respond—created what was observed as the next theme.

7

Finding Equanimity: Strategies for Well-Being

Life is parallel to hell, but I must maintain.
(Nasir Jones, 1994)

I often say to myself, and sometimes to others, "*The world is unrelentingly fascinating.*" This small statement, which I use in moments of triumph or disaster, always brings me back to balance, and no matter how brief it is, I find comfort in those following moments. While sharing space with these men, it felt like their well-being was in constant need of protection. And as my mind met their experience, I visualized their mental life as a fort, with much of the space outside decorated with marred foxhole covers and other defensive fighting positions. Sitting across from them, I envisioned the constant enemy activity that created the battered landscape that in turn told me the story of the forever war at the walls. But any mindful observer could clearly see the effort and desire to protect what was held dear on the inside. While this may very well be my own craving to project my experience onto them, you should know that all of us found our well-being as something that needed to actively be protected and we would engage in a variety of creative strategies to do so. From my conversations, three strategies emerged: close your circle, engage in mental and physical maintenance, and strong Black identity.

Close Your Circle

For most of the men I spoke to, maintaining their well-being often meant reducing their interactions with those who displayed negative or neutral responses to the murders of Black people. For Oscar, that meant staying home, "I wasn't leaving my house. I refused." Additionally, the majority of Black men I interviewed specifically needed to isolate themselves from people or situations that overtly supported former President Trump out of a fear that they were knowingly racist or unknowingly supporting racist systems, "People will say . . . I voted for, for, for him. I say, I am sure you did. . . . I mean, now I lost so many [friends], [well] they weren't really friends" (Oscar).

Black men also protected themselves by reducing their media consumption. This meant taking time away from social media hubs or limiting their exposure to some news networks because, as Niles said, "a lot of times with the media it's like it's always something else, you know," meaning there is always another atrocity happening to someone who looks like you. In addition, the way the media discusses these atrocities is often untrue and leaves Black men feeling enraged and invalidated. Atukwei provided a specific example: "Even the riots and how [the media] portrayed . . . the Black folks . . . who actually were protesting peacefully. [It] wasn't the Black folks that were looting rioting . . . but [the media] portrayed it." As a result, my interviewees limited who they spoke to about their experience for fear of being mischaracterized. For Niles, the only reason he spoke to me was because of our familial bond, "[You are] the only person I will probably do this with, right. Because I trust you, you, my family, and I know you're going to be careful in how if you're going to quote me in something, or how you're putting that out."

An overall lack of trust is what kept us safe for so long. And sadly, it is what many feel they need to continue to do, and it's for good reason.

Physical/Mental Health Maintenance

Black men also engaged in physical exercise and ate healthy foods as strategies for well-being during the twin-pandemic. For Oscar, that meant going for walks with his wife, and for Marcel, it was planning times for workouts, "I'll try to do small things to make myself happy . . . stuff like hit the gym." Niles implemented a routine of exercise and dieting, "I worked out, I started taking care of my body, eatin' right." Additionally, with a background in sports, Niles uniquely leveraged his athletic experience by comparing achieving well-being during the twin-pandemic to the difficult journey of success in sports, "I look at it like when you're working out, this muscle was hurting right now. [Matt: Yeah.] . . . But the result when you win that race. [Matt: Yeah.] The result when you win that game it's all for it when you win the championship." Additionally, during the twin-pandemic individuals were not opposed to expressing themselves by talking about their difficulties. Such as receiving professional help, "I started therapy," (Izaak), or talking to close friends about topics, "if it's a conversation I need to have that's a little more intimate . . . like for someone that [I'm] close with."

"King Kunta": Strong Black Identity

For my interviewees, a strong sense of who they were as Black men was meaningful for their confidence. In addition, it was a buffer against their fears of being stereotyped and a way to resist offensive narratives about Black people. As Oscar put it, "I am so pro-Black people I probably scare people." Because these Black men were comfortable with their Black masculine identities, they could not only resist these negative messages but also leverage their comfort with their skin, their community, and their Black lineage to combat adversity. Niles told me, "One of the things that my father gave me that he doesn't even realize is, be who you say you're going to be all the time. . . . Same way I'm talking to you right now is the same way I talk in the boardroom, [or] in the hood. . . . I only know one way to be." Furthermore, Niles's strong Black identity protected his well-being from threats regarding how White friends and co-workers may perceive the intersection of his race and masculinity as well, "If I want to cry in the boardroom and make myself vulnerable there, I'm gone do that . . . and you not going make me out to be weak because I did that, because I'm strong."

Expressing the emotion of anger was complex for these Black men, particularly in a work environment. Marcel noted: "You don't want to be seen as like the angry black man," so dealing with systemic racism required creative coping strategies. During the twin-pandemic some individuals, such as Atukwei, found the time to express his racial identity development through songwriting,

> I, have a song called [song name]. And literally . . . the words say "heartbroken, don't know how to mend it." And it literally comes from my experiences as a child because that's how I felt like my heart was broken and I didn't know how to mend it. But literally that song is all about my experience, kind of growing up in America.

For Atukwei, songwriting has been a way for him to process how he's had to "collude with oppression" while still maintaining a strong Black identity to survive in America,

> Figuring out, oh wow, like I got a, I got, you know to be the good nigger, for people to treat me nice or for people [to not see me] as a threat and all those things, right? I'm having to learn this in high school and middle school. . . . And then seeing just

> how all the Black kids are getting sent to the principal's office and all these other things and literally happens to collude because of how I see my peers being treated like fuck I don't wanna be treated like that, you know. So yeah, man (laughs).

Lastly, it was heavy for me to find out that many of them talked about difficulty communicating with same-race peers who were in earlier phases of Black identity such as preencounter, who forwarded colorblind ideologies and denied racism. I felt this way not because of some sort of *holier than thou* experience, but a sad relatability which I felt alongside them. The men I spoke to were comfortable with their Black identity and aware of our country's racial history and current problems, and just as their identities were unique, so were their responses. Some such as Zahair continued to engage with those who denied present racism; others like Atukwei distanced himself from them; and Oscar, Niles, and Marcel focused on systemic change, for the betterment of all, rather than individual communication with them.

Nobody is an island, and as a result, a large part of any identity development often involves help from others who share an identity with you but have already done the work of developing a strong identity. In this case I mean that Black men are often assisted in the development of their Black masculine identity by other Black men who have established a strong Black masculine identity for themselves. This is not meant to be touted as a position of superiority, rather a responsibility. It's a communal approach that invites shepherdship. It simultaneously serves as protection from a strong role model, while also allowing for the transmission of acceptance and wisdom of another while the person develops a comfort with who they are.

However, the mentor's own well-being is not always addressed in this process, which brings me back to the feeling of sadness I'd like to expand on. I am writing during a time in our country in which we remain surrounded by racial trauma, and the threat of White supremacy looms as the biggest terrorist in our country (Department of Homeland Security, 2020). The added stress of the twin-pandemic made me notice that many people I would consider to be Black mentors sometimes needed to take a step back for their own well-being. And what makes me sad is just how much sense that makes. After all, what can be more hurtful than speaking to a young Black man who doesn't believe racism exists while you, their racial kin, see the familiar puppeteer's strings, threaded in White supremacy, firmly attached to his limbs, forcing him to dance a dance of self-targeted degradation, which he believes is his own doing, all while enduring your own daily slashes from the oppressive whip that was the twin-pandemic? Speaking for myself, sometimes I just could not find the strength.

Interpretations and Synthesis

Black identity has been shown to be a protective factor against discrimination (Oliver et al., 2017); and what I found most filling was how these men used their Black identity proactively. Before any obstacle would arise, they knew that they would be able to garner a mindset for victory. For example, they often referenced their own definition of what it means to be a Black man in America, which often included some form of overcoming struggle. When obstacles such as COVID-19, social injustice, or the intersection of both surfaced, they leveraged this identity as a reminder that they knew they could survive.

Additionally, while Black men were feeling the effects of racism, the very existence of racism was called into question. As a result, these men not only needed to deal with the negative effects of racism but also needed to find ways to manage their well-being through widely publicized scrutiny of their lived pain. As mentioned, the Black men I spoke to leaned on three approaches. The first was to close their circle, excluding a majority of White men or women who did not believe or validate their experiences of systemic racism and social injustice. They searched for clues to identify these people and spaces through political merchandise such as Make America Great Again (MAGA) slogans, Confederate flags, politicized talking points, or participation in noninclusive social movements such as Blue Lives Matter. Additionally, they cut ties with news networks or media sources that were White-centric. By this I mean they did not subject themselves to news outlets that they felt, knowingly or otherwise, accepted forms of White supremacy and consequently did not accurately report Black experiences. Instead, they sought out counternarratives, which are a significant component for undoing oppression and understanding the experience of the oppressed.

8

Brothers and Sisters in Trauma: Black Support and Scrutiny

See, to live is to suffer but to survive
Well, that's to find meaning in the suffering
(Earl Simmons, 1998, citing Allport, 1946)

Around the time I decided to write this book—after much needed encouragement from people I trust—I relocated from Kansas to Nashville, Tennessee. I had never been there, or more accurately here. As I'm writing to you from my hand-me-down bed in my far-too-costly apartment that a graduate student, such as myself, can barely afford, but was the cheapest available. Finding cheaper housing farther away may have been possible; however, I wanted to live close to where I would be working because I was afraid of what I call the "unknown inevitabilities." It's the inevitable shit that happens to you that you can't always see coming, but you know is out there. For some, this may be your car not starting or bad traffic, but for my Black ass it was more about having to pay—literally and figuratively—to potentially live next to racists. For many Black people, this is a significant consideration when moving. And in this day and age, relocating to a politically red state has become a cause for caution already. So on the day I arrived, and I approached the billboard that hung off of Highway 24 that read "Nashville loves Trump," my anxiety was exacerbated, as I feared I was going it alone.

However, I was thankful that the same day I met a great man. An older Black farmer who didn't know me, but I like to think he knew I could use a friend, specifically a Black one. I had never had a friend who farmed, and with my parents both being raised in poverty in Baltimore, Maryland, I didn't learn a ton about vegetable growing, or eating. I don't blame my parents for this because all their life their job was to hustle. As a result, when my sister and brothers were born and they hustled to get out of Baltimore, like a family business, we inherited those same values and skills. The farmer I met also hustled all his life. However, hustling in the city is different than hustling on the farm. So in a new location, and with a new friend, I had a new opportunity to learn, and so I did. I learned about how the properties of basil work as an anti-inflammatory. I learned the best way to grill okra, and how to make green tomatoes actually delicious. Laughs, drinks and candid conversations about race and the world would continue as the days went by. However, what was most remarkable was that before we ever spoke words, there was an unspoken truth between us: we needed to support each other.

It's been said that since the first slaves touched down at what was then called Point Comfort, Virginia, in 1619, they were already brothers and sisters in trauma. Four centuries later, during the twin-pandemic, we received yet another example of these roots, both communal like my example above, as well as scrutiny born from a scarcity mindset that our culture teaches Black people. As I have begun to show you, these Black men experienced their well-being in a variety of ways, and this extended to their relationships with other Black men and women. Some talked to me about instances of support from Black people, and others shared the scrutiny they received. Those who received support from same-race peers, whether they shared the same beliefs or not, told me more about their feeling of comfort and acceptance than those who experienced scrutiny from their same-race peers. The latter often needed to find subsequent reserves of resilience in their Black masculine identity.

The racial atrocities of recent years had such a visceral impact on some of the men I spoke to and on members of their social circles that they chose to go to therapy. Izaak knew he specifically wanted a Black therapist. When I asked him why, he said that he felt he could receive "comfort" and "a safe space because even if [he] had a feeling or a thought that was maybe not of the norm . . . [they're not going to] judge [him] for it." Others found comfort from Black mentors in their lives. Oscar explained, "My mentor and I, we talked a lot during this time." They often spoke with reverence for the people who helped them process specific incidents, such as Breonna Taylor's and George Floyd's murders and a lingering fear at the time that Derek Chauvin would not be charged with Floyd's murder. Oscar noted the role of his mentor in helping him process Ahmaud Arbery's murder: "To see [him] shot like a dog, right? . . . And then to find out that, that three or four prosecutors had turn it, turned it down . . . that's when I, I talked to my mentor." Time and time again, strong Black mentors proved to be helpful.

And as a father and husband, Oscar works with his wife to create space at home for the expression and processing of conversations about racial injustice. Oscar told me how his wife responded when they watched George Floyd choked on TV, "[My] wife came up and stood beside me. I think that's what helped me too. My wife came up and look[ed] at it. And we just stood there watch[ed] the TV and we didn't say a word."

Individuals who did not have Black mentors found refuge with others who held a BIPOC identity, as Marcel explained: "I have a mentor in my life who has been in my life since I was in high school. And he's a Mexican-American. . . . He's the only one I was ever able to relate to in these moments."

This positive experience extended to other Black relationships as well, creating a communal experience for them. Some Black men identified moments of comfortable expression, as in the case of Oscar: "Bruh man, me and my cousin we talked a lot. . . . I talked to people in athletics and, you know, we all felt the same way . . . we're tired of this shit." Having same-race peers to vent with and talk to was important for these Black men. Some, such as Zahair, recognized this and wanted to provide such opportunities not only for himself, but also for others,

> I did a Juneteenth cookout . . . We raised the money [from] the community. Like everyone, like a lot of people donated like twenty bucks. We were able to get like chicken, hot dogs, you know, things like that. We got a park we worked with the [city name] community. They helped us or whatever. . . . And we tried to do as much as we can with [COVID-19] like, we had little temperature checkers. We had face mask[s], like we had hand sanitizer. [You] know [with people swapping shifts] and everything like that, you know, [to] try to mitigate as much as possible. But it was like one of those things where it's like everything is so low, and everything's so down we need like something to, to raise people's morales.

Among their stories, joy was often seen as plentiful. It was an abundant feeling they wanted to savor for themselves and spread to others. In fact, it was like the success of other

Black people was liberating for these Black men, as Oscar noted: "Seeing my grandson graduate from high school, man. . . . He's my son's son. And you know . . . when we lost our son, bruh, I was ready to go . . . and to see [him] make it, ahh, [it] was special." In line with the success of Black people was their safety and well-being. For Zahair, who is a pacifist, it is a commitment, "So when I say Black lives matter, I mean, like all Black lives, you know like women, children, gay, whatever . . . your life still matters, you know, like you might not be into politics . . . [but] every Black person on this earth matters." Because of COVID-19, finding connections required creativity. For example, Atukwei discussed the positive impact of his virtual group of Black men. In this virtual space, full of educators and corporate leaders, processing experiences was a part of their conversations; however, talking about what they were doing to take care of themselves tended to take center stage:

> I talk[ed] to my brothers. . . . And I remember when the [twin-pandemic] was happening, we all just kinda got on like Zooms in different groups and just check in with each other. And it was very interesting because folks were not really processing the incidents very much. In a way, for me, I always think about [the] "how" because we see these incidents so much and we know at this point we're all kinda just very much aware of the

> society we live in. You know, what, what the outcomes are for people with dark skin color.

Just as its members displayed cognitive flexibility, so too did the conversation topics, which melded toward what the group needed, "Do we need to, to just have Zoom happy hours? (laughs)"

The sense of family in these interviews was vast, regardless of blood relation. Zahair noted, "I hadn't met a [Black] community yet where the sense of family wasn't like big, like mom, dad, grandma, aunties, cousins coming over . . . oh this my uncle, and it's my dad's really close friend." This expansive experience of family allowed Black men to have conversations with Black male peers about wide arrays of topics, including their fears. Zahair continued:

> My friend . . . He's like, he's like this huge, like play football [player], big guy. He was just like, yeah man I don't know bro, I kinda just give up man because it's like, like what, what can we do even when we do the right thing, something bad happens and if we do the wrong things something bad happens, He's like, I just don't know at this point how to feel about anything.

These moments of intimate connection were powerful for both the person sharing and the person or people receiving the messages. However, not all interactions were rejuvenating.

Scarcity Mindset

One difficulty experienced by some of the men I spoke to was criticism from their same-race peers. In these interactions I could feel the disappointment and frustration in the lack of support or outright desire to see the other fail. Niles told me how he noticed this dynamic within his own relationships and others in the Black community who do not treat each other with love:

> You [always] see people talk about, well, Black folk done had it worse and we this, that, and the other, but here I am when I deal with you . . . you don't even deal with me right. [Matt: Mmm.]. You don't even love, you don't even listen. . . . I'm saying, why we ain't loving each other? Why If I got a business, why you gotta . . . speak bad about me?

Marcel experienced this negative dynamic in his own circles as well. As he tried to navigate his career in a predominantly White institution (PWI), which already took a blow to his well-being, he was also receiving blowback from Black people in his life, "They're like, oh man, stop going out there working with those rich White folks. Come back [to us].” During our interview, I tried to provide an interpretation of his position to gain a better understanding, which he agreed with,

> Matt: It feels like this really shitty dynamic that you're stuck in where, for you to . . . make enough money financially means to some Black people that you're sort of abandoning them. And in actuality that's not [it], you're trying to carry them with you in different ways and immerse those people who don't know the stories of Black people [and their] systemic struggles with information in DEI meetings and things like this. [Marcel: Yeah].

This position was exhausting to him, and he tried to combat their perception of him as a sellout by instead reminding himself of the meaning and impact he is having on the “future leaders of our country” at his PWI. “I like think I gave them a sense of reality.” Marcel felt like he was actively popping the racial bubble created at his institution and believed he was helping to provide holistic education for the students. However, his same-race peers and family responded critically to his actions, “My friends and my family, like, you know, they'll like shun me or whatever, like oh, you know, you out there like aiding the enemy.” When I asked how he feels about this dynamic he responded, “I won't lie, [it] caused me to just internalize much more, shut down much more."

I asked those who had received negative messages from same-race peers if they had a positive experience speaking with me as a Black man who accepted their situation and pursuits. Both Marcel and Niles shared an appreciation that I was thankful, relieved, and encouraged to hear. Niles said, "You know, you have a powerful voice, man. And in talking to you, you're, you don't even understand. You're helping me in my, in my therapeutic mindset."

Interpretations and Synthesis

Trauma bonding is commonly used to point to the dynamic that takes place when a victim of prolonged abuse emotionally bonds with the perpetrator of that abuse (Hopper, 2017; Reid et al., 2013). It's often used now to describe an experience victims of kidnappings may have toward their kidnapper. However, whenever I hear about trauma bonding I think back to when I read the *Narrative of the Life of Fredrick Douglass.* He wrote about the bonds many of his fellow slaves formed with those who had enslaved them. He described how these bonds were sometimes so powerful he would see other enslaved people defending their enslaver's honor by arguing or getting in physical fights with enslaved people from other plantations to proclaim that their master was better. I think it's this dynamic that still exists today, that hurts me most. There is no one with the title of *master* present in our country, but the antiquated systems that were born of White supremacy still have a strong pulse. So for me, seeing Black men defending these systems is a contemporary version of seeing the slave defend the whip. Sometimes it's only from a distance that I can stomach it. Guided by the slave master mindset, my racial kin who are willing to embody their role of inferiority look like ghosts of histories past, rebirthed. I can't help but see dark-skinned revenants who once stood vanguard to the same whip that tore their skin now return, in ideology, to defend the systems it created. It's barely hyperbole for me to say this breaks my heart.

Another form of scrutiny adjacent to the defense of systems was hoping for other Black people to fail. A couple of the men I spoke to felt like other Black people sometimes tried to tear them down rather than build them up. This reminded me of crabs in a barrel, a saying I'd often hear growing up about how some Black people would treat each other. If you were to put crabs into a barrel, they will try to climb out, but they never make it because the other crabs will grab their legs and pull them down. Essentially if I can't succeed, neither can you. I never really liked this saying, not because I find it offensive—I just find it shortsighted. Trauma can do a lot to a person's brain and behavior, and this statement neglects that fact. When you find yourself trapped in a cage of someone else's doing, you are terrified. Especially if the rules of the barrel are that only one can get out. That is what created the scarcity mindset. So it's not that these men or women want other Black people to fail, it's that they want to succeed but know our world's rules do not allow for all of them to make it out.

So, instead of making Black people out to be on par with crabs, ask yourself why you needed to put them in a barrel and create these rules in the first place. It's the denial of this contextual understanding that always saddens me when I hear White people say things like, "Well, Black people need to stop killing each other" or "It's not my fault they're burning their own neighborhoods." Or my least favorite, "Slavery was so long ago, get over it." They just don't see it: the presence of continued trauma their ancestors created, and they now protect. As I said, underneath the crab mentality is the fear that only a limited number of Black people are allowed to make it, so one person's success marks the closing of a door for another. Sadly, the limitations of Black success due to racism in hiring and promotion continue to be a harsh truth for Black Americans (Pincus, 2019). Further, these inequalities are reinforced by high-profile examples such as the performative interview extended to former NFL head coach Brian Flores who was brought in for an interview with the Denver Broncos so that the team could meet the minimum requirement of interviewing a person of color, despite having already filled the position (Vrentas & Belson, 2022).

In sum, the scrutiny within Black communities exhausted these men. It left some feeling like they were "sellouts" and left others frustrated in our struggle to love each other. Noticeable in my interviews, however, was an awareness by these men of systemic inequities that created situations that in turn pitted Black people against each other for physical and psychological survival. This awareness speaks to the men's well-developed Black identity.

Trauma Bonding: Remix

I want you to try on a different frame for understanding our experience. Through victimization we have become survivors and created, as a result of generations of trauma, a collective strength that is branded into Black culture. This new frame, sometimes referred to as posttraumatic growth (PTG), (Ortega-Williams et al., 2021), allows us to hone in on the positive adjustments we have made to cope with trauma. As you read earlier in this chapter, Black support often provided an injection of life. It allowed these Black men to feel comfortable sharing intimate experiential topics and beliefs with each other. This includes their fears related to specific atrocities and the effect they were having on their everyday lives. Additionally, it provided a space of foundational resonance, empathy, and laughter that begat additional ways for Black people to come together or gain the confidence needed to seek professional help. While these spaces embraced conversations related to COVID-19 and social injustice, they were also opportunities to escape or be authentic. These communal spaces provided momentary reprieve for these Black men. Additionally, it was in the depths of these conversations about shared Black relationships that I heard the most joyous experiences. Participants expressed joy in seeing other Black people succeed and desire to actively support their peers. Many wished for my own success as the interviewer, telling me to stay in touch in case I need anything, or if I'm in town to know I have a place to stay. This, to me, spoke volumes about the extension of family within Black culture and community.

9
Talking to White People

I wonder if they'll laugh when I am dead?
Why am I fighting to live, if I'm just living to fight?
Why am I trying to see, when there ain't nothing in sight?
Why am I trying to give, when no one gives me a try?
Why am I dying to live, if I'm just living to die?
(Tupac Shakur & Christopher Wallace,
2003, citing Winter, 1971)

It seems like every election cycle brings out the worst in us as people, and although I'm too young to remember what elections were like before social media, I can only imagine how much worse it has gotten. Now with technology, we use our phones and computers to throw stones at each other. Then we turn to our same news outlets for sanctuary in the ideas they gave us to begin with. Writers and anchors whose job it is to *spin* topics that involve the lives of real people soothe our beliefs that in some cases are the manifestation of our own insecurities. This feels like a time-honored tradition in our country; however, it feels fair to say that the 2020 election was different. Truth and facts were put into question by every political party in a way I had never seen before. However, after I sat and listened to Trevor Noah's interview with author Timothy Snyder about fascism and tyranny, I finally had language for what I observed taking place in our country. I specifically remembered him saying the following:

> If you want to rip the heart out of a democracy directly, if you want to go right at it and kill it, what you do is you go after facts. And that is what modern authoritarians do. Step one: You lie yourself, all the time. Step two: You say it's your opponents and the journalists who lie. Step three: Everyone looks around and says, "What is truth? There is no truth." And then, resistance is impossible, and the game is over.

Before I saw this interview, I was exploring this during the twin-pandemic. As a researcher and psychologist, I am privileged to have the training to examine where news outlets get their information, as we are often the creators and suppliers of that information. So, perhaps with curiosity as my superpower, I intentionally listened to and read everything from political talking points to research studies from all gradations of political affiliation. Not to find some sort of absolute truth but instead to see, as we say in my culture, whose shit stinks. And in conversations with some of my White friends, it was like they stunk and didn't even realize it.

Online or in person, it felt like some White people would talk as if they knew the taste of the ocean after having plunged their heads into fishbowls. I noticed that they only chose to receive or pursue information that aligned with their beliefs and soothed their insecurities. This rigidity, created by their own entitlement, infuriated many Black men because we would see many of them argue about topics that held our people on trial. I have no reservations in saying that it was a justifiable anger as we saw White people sit atop a self-appointed judge's bench and state verdicts like, "He should have listened to the officers," followed by some sort of computer slang laugh or sneer and shrug before saying, "I'm just stating facts." For me, their laughs haunted my mind like unfortunate background music that played as I saw the bodies of Ahmaud, George, Breonna, Jacob, and the ongoing list of 243 Black men killed by police in just one year (Statista, 2022). So, I remind myself to breathe.

And upon exhaling, I'd like to address a question you may be wondering: Why am I talking about politics to start off a chapter about White people? Because in the 2020 election especially, there were clear candidates and followers who were without question previously and presently racist, and many White people—57 percent to be precise—decorated their bodies, homes, minds, and ballots with them. So, I say that to say if you did and you're feeling offended because it sounds like I'm calling you racist, allow me to reprise a Dave Chappelle line as my rebuttal, "All right, [White people], fine. You are not a [racist]. But you are wearing a [racist's] uniform." So you'll have to excuse my distance.

Our systems of racial oppression were created by and maintained by White people who held Whiteness, as a construct, at the core of their development of these systems. Because of this, it was important to include Black men's experiences of their interactions with White peers. Please walk with me and acknowledge the stark contrast in feelings and responses depending on what White people did. When White people displayed a lack of awareness, the Black men distanced themselves. When White people demonstrated accountability and recognition, the Black men found comfort.

White Lack of Awareness=Distancing

This subtheme points to the dominant response of Black men to distance themselves when engaging with White peers who displayed through words, actions, or visible political merchandise what felt like either a lack of awareness or an explicit denial of the plight of Black people in this country. For example, Atukwei discussed with me a conversation with a former White friend,

> I have like this one particular friend and I'm like you're lowkey a racist. . . . Here's why I would

> not want to be around you. Because if I'm around you and these things are happening, I would be fearful of my life because of how you think, because of how you perceive the situation, [because] of just your lack of willingness to acknowledge that this shit is real. And so that's how some of the conversations have been with some of those individuals is that I blatantly would tell them like I can't be around you. Because if I get pulled over, and these things are going on in my mind or emotionally, I'm having a psycho-physiological like reaction in my body and my mind and you can't even understand what might be going on. Because you think, oh, like this cop is a good cop. I don't care if they're a good cop or a bad cop, but like understanding what might be going on for me is important for me, for you to acknowledge what emotional state I might be in. The fact that you can't recognize that, I was like I can't be around you.

Atukwei had to assert a boundary in order for these White individuals to have a "light bulb" moment of realizing the severity of their lack of awareness.

Additionally, some Black men grew exhausted with feeling as though they had to "collude" with oppressive systems and placate or console White individuals for the guilt they experienced. Zahair explained: "The White people, (deep exhale) like they were kind of scared to say like . . . what can I do to help? And it's like, do you want the real answer?" In those moments Zahair wanted to fully express himself: "Send your kids to Black schools, that will help, get funding in the Black schools," as well as desiring for them to not be idle when in spaces that are promoting discrimination:

> I wish I could be like okay . . . if you really want change, you have to completely cut this people off . . . The reason why those people won't change, and their kids won't change is because you let it slide . . . like [oh] that's just them . . . Uncle Ben just does that. It's like no, Uncle Ben's a racist, bro. Like tell him to stop that or cut him off.

However, Zahair's environments and circumstances were not always safe enough to be able to express this, so instead he recognized that he needed to become smaller to accommodate:

> Like you kinda had to tell them like, oh no is not you . . . You kinda have to break it down to them like . . . it's like your grandparents, who they vote for, and . . . your auntie who says the slick racist stuff. . . . They're in charge of hiring somebody, so some dude didn't get a job because,

> you know auntie [name], is super racist . . . I know it's not you, but it's them.

Atukwei had a similar experience of trying to manage White guilt in his life, "White co-workers I think always came from a place of guilt. . . . I, I didn't know how to entertain those conversations. . . . I don't know how to sit there and listen to [them] talk about what they're feeling . . . the magnitude of emotions is completely different." Particularly noting how their sudden realization of the justice system does him little good, he explained, "You having an open eye of the justice system is very different than my experience of [America]." Additionally, In the instances where he would try to have conversations with White peers about BLM protests, he noticed a disheartening experience in which his White friends, who identified as Republican, were quick to absorb negative depictions of Black people from the media. Moreover, regardless of challenging their beliefs with facts and firsthand experience, it was dismissed,

> I had a few White friends who are Republican. . . . They eat it up, no matter how many facts I send to them, no matter how many articles or videos, or even me being in a protest and showing them videos of a peaceful protest no matter what it was. They just want to cling on to what the media is saying about the negative side.

After making himself vulnerable and trying to engage, for his own mental state he had to give up, "I quit trying. I quit trying and I got, I don't know how many DMs back and forth that I've engaged with fact to fact to fact, fact to fact to fact. At some point it gets exhausting."

The workplaces of these Black men were also very much entrenched in efforts to maintain racist systems. This again led to distancing from co-workers or even having to resign from jobs during the global health pandemic. For example, when substantial efforts were not taken to recognize and rectify racism in his workplace, Atukwei explored financing strategies to see if he could leave his career for something more comfortable: "[The pandemic] really shaped the trajectory of my career in a different direction. . . . The pandemic brought on nuanced challenges that [were] tied to my identity." This led him to contemplate, "Do I still stay in this role because I need that money to live? Or do I make the decision to figure out what are my finances look like?"

Other men tried to fight singlehandedly against the system but encountered demoralizing realizations. For example, Marcel was asked to serve on his school's diversity, equity, and inclusion (DEI) team, initially thinking it could be a space for seeds of change to be planted; instead, it became a refuge for White guilt and a factory for racial performativity. This led to him fearing that they were doing it just to "check off boxes." Furthermore, his school meetings did not show an intention to be areas of racial understanding or systemic growth toward equity. In fact, these meetings actively engaged teachers and faculty with avoidance interventions for race-related topics by offering scripts saying that "when you hear kids talking about [race or racism] . . . you shouldn't let [them] talk about these things and this is how you should like redirect them." This had a noticeable effect on Marcel's well-being, "That [pissed] me off man, that pissed me off. . . . [It was] the first time I started to question if what I'm doing was right? And even to this day . . . I don't even know." For Marcel and Atukwei, leaving their job was constantly in consideration. As Atukwei explained, "There are times when I'm just like man I wanna go back home and live in Ghana. . . . You're constantly thinking about your identity in spaces you walk in, what's collusion going to look like? . . . How am I going to survive in this space, you know? Who are my allies, who are my foes?" This was a shared reality of what it meant to be a Black man in America, especially during the twin-pandemic, "figuring out how you're going to survive, because . . . you never know who's going to be against you because of the color of your skin."

White Accountability and Recognition

Juxtaposed to experiences with White individuals who showed a lack of awareness were social experiences with White peers who showed accountability or recognition of racial atrocities and continued systemic racism. These experiences often led Black men to feel more comfortable being around these peers and in some instances seeing White accountability or acknowledgment provided a significant cathartic release.

An acknowledgment or awareness of sociopolitical events and systems connected to race went a long way in Black and White relationships. Both Izaak and Oscar shared a higher comfort being around White peers who had this awareness. Izaak had two such friends: "One's a gay White man. And the other [is] just like this middle-aged [guy]. . . . They both have some sensors, the wherewithal or this awareness to me." Marcel provided a thorough articulation of the powerful impact his White co-workers had on him by reaching out, "I had two people . . . check on me and how I felt being like a Black man in America right now are saying like, you know, they're with me, or their sorry. Or If I need a hug . . . and both times I like cried." Although it was some time ago, he retold the stories of these individuals with such detail that it was like it happened yesterday,

> It was actually a new person who was part of my team. And she was like, hey, I don't know if I'm overstepping, but you know, like I just want to make sure you're okay, like being a Black man today, like how are you feeling? And, you know, I'm here. And I just broke down and she just like hugged me and later I apologized for it, but I didn't realize, how much those little things mean.

> You know cause it wasn't happening. So since it wasn't happening, whatever I was harboring just kept sitting there and I didn't realize it . . . [because] you just run through your normal routine . . . and [she] was like, how are you today? I'm like, yeah, I'm not good. I'm not okay.

While he appreciated his coworker's empathy, Marcel noted that he continued to practice indifference to protect himself, "[It] felt different. Felt very indifferent. [Matt: mmm.] I hadn't experienced it, so at first it threw me off."

His second experience happened a few months later. One of his supervisors approached him after one of the aforementioned school meetings directed toward avoiding conversations about race.

> I remember walking out feeling super like infuriated really. And as I was walking out, [name], she was there, standing and she just put her hand on my shoulder. And she was just like, I'm so sorry, I think of you every day and I can't imagine how you feel and she like forced me to hug her and I just like stood there crying, and everyone walked out the meeting, see me there crying. And no one ever asked why or anything like that after that.

Interpretations and Synthesis

> I picked the cotton,
> and I carried it to market,
> and I built the railroads,
> under someone else's whip, for nothing.
> (Baldwin, 1965)

Out of every theme, I saw perhaps the starkest distinction here. Before I give you my long interpretation and synthesis of what happened, I want to state succinctly the dynamic that took place: White peers of all sorts—friends, coworkers, and the like—who showed a lack of racial awareness, denied systemic racism, or promoted of political/sociopolitical messages that showed racial insensitivity were distanced or removed from Black men's lives. However, White peers who articulated an accountability or recognition of systemic racism, social injustice, and the continued plight of Black Americans were much more valued and remained in their circles or were invited in. Now, I would like to ask for your patience, because for me to address the former with you, I need to go back in time decades prior.

In the year 1965, one hundred years after the abolition of slavery, creative means to disenfranchise Black people were already thoroughly entrenched in America (Blessett, 2015; Howard, 2008), and at their core was the idea, implicit or otherwise, of Black inferiority. As I mentioned earlier, this idea had long been promulgated by ethically perverse works, which became literature accepted by America's White population and its consequent systems (Degruy, 2017). It was in this year that our country saw, on the highest of academic stages, a debate between civil rights activist James Baldwin and writer William F. Buckley Jr. on "race." I wanted to highlight this moment in time to allude to the similarities shared between then and now. It is important we do not run from the parallel themes of condescension articulated by Buckley toward Baldwin that day and our present situation.

The debate, taking place at the prestigious Cambridge University Union between a Black and White man, was unheard of because of the lack of credence given any Black person's thoughts. As author of *The Fire is Upon Us* Nicholas Buccola puts it, being a Black man at that time meant not having your ideas taken seriously. So when Buckley stated, "It is impossible, in my judgment, to deal with the indictment of Mr. Baldwin unless one is prepared to deal with him as a White man" (Brockell, 2019), he was in essence saying I'm going to pretend you are White so I can take you seriously. Likewise, today's racial climate and narrative subtly jabs at Black men and women, blame for their struggles in America as a consequential result of their own lethargy and incompetence.

As we return to present day, in this study it was clear that Black men did not feel safe being in relationships with

White people who denied racism existed or who supported racially insensitive movements (such as Blue Lives Matter) or policies such as differential treatment in policing. Some of those I interviewed needed to leave their jobs due to a lack of racial sensitivity or racial identity awareness from coworkers. The majority of Black men did not articulate vested interest in developing relationships with White people who denied racism out of a recognition that it would be at the risk of their well-being and not the other person's. It is my interpretation that deniers of racial inequality, who knowingly or otherwise align with Buckleyesque rhetoric, have the freedom to do so without bearing the cognitive, emotional, and interpersonal load faced by those who are subjected to racial inequalities. Moreover, they have the privilege of returning to their daily lives surrounded by systems that actively work for them. It is in recognition of this dynamic that my interviewees, other Black men, and I often disengaged.

However, not all Black men had the flexibility to depart these systems. For instance, Marcel was financially tethered to his job and was stuck feeling tortured by its structure. I would like to reflect on Marcel's experience of being tokenized in a system that attempted to be color blind by using two tenets from CRT: interest convergence and structural determinism. His school system actively avoided conversations about race while simultaneously using his racial identity as a means to meet demographic quotas. Further, it was not until a year and a half into the twin-pandemic that his school created a diversity, equity, and inclusion (DEI) committee, which ultimately felt performative by its inability to create structural changes in the institution. The dance Marcel experienced is predictable, and we can extrapolate it to the larger issues in our country. Despite DEI committees existing long before the twin-pandemic, his school did not create a committee until it became a popularized talking point nationwide such that the failure to have one could result in negative public relations. When schools or other organizations create DEI committees under the guise of racial support they are able to marry their interest to the accepted public perception, rather than engaging in change for virtuosity. In this, their goal is not to alleviate oppressive systems but to save themselves. Such action will always result in a predictable destination: new ways to oppress.

Like many of my participants, I have served on multiple DEI committees, so I will speak unapologetically for the sake of encouraging compassionate change. In my candid experience, had I not been a member of the DEI committees at their inception, I would have thought they had been pillaged. What I mean by this is that the systems, which were created by and for White people, without accountability, sought not to undo wrongs but instead to keep these systems in power. As such, I've found that many of these structures are gilded at best, where any amount of creative brilliance within the committees is frequently stifled by the inherent, intentional lack of power within them. In my experience, it has felt as though the individuals and groups who benefit from the status quo work tirelessly to keep education on race and racism inaccessible, as evident in current legislation banning the discussion of race in schools.[6]

Additionally, in many cases, the actions of even well-intentioned White people will have their outcomes already determined as insufficient or harmful because of their racial miseducation. Furthermore, BIPOC and White allies will find themselves, at best, encumbered or limited by existing systemic racial barriers established from policy officials. Marcel's example of school meetings and DEI committee meetings articulated this point, where regardless of the intention of DEI members, the school meetings actively worked against DEI efforts by focusing on how to avoid discussions about race among students, even providing specific interventions in case such conversations were happening.

In contrast, the dynamic between Black men and their White peers who supported them through historical awareness and active recognition or active dismantling of systems was much different. These Black men stated or alluded to increased comfort with White individuals who did this. Some felt comfortable enough to engage in critical

---

[6] As per Ray and Gibbons 2021, "The legislations mostly ban the discussion, training, and/or orientation that the U.S. is inherently racist as well as any discussions about conscious and unconscious bias, privilege, discrimination, and oppression."

conversations about race-related topics or even to invite them to community spaces with their Black peers. At the same time while some felt increased comfort around these White peers, they still would not engage in critical conversations. When these men were asked further why they would not engage, they expressed a reluctance born from a fear that the White peers were not genuine in their interest. Some feared that these White people want "to be performative or be perceived as "nice" White people. With existing literature having explored the harm of performative allyship on social justice movements (Kalina, 2020) and this book going further to articulate the direct impact it has on Black men's well-being, I'd like to close where we began.

If you hold a White identity, I'm asking you to ask yourself if you will laugh at my pain. And if your answer falls easily in the negative, I'll ask for your patience, because I have had many experiences of White people lying about their virtue. As a result, I needed to find grounding and safety in the sagacity of leaders like Baldwin, who articulated my justifiable experience: "I don't believe what you say, because I see what you do." So you must show and continue to show me something else. I guess what I'm trying to tell you is I don't want you to do this work so we can be friends, I want you to do this because you've realized it's right. Then maybe in seeing what you do, routinely, we will become close.

10

Generalized Social Experiences

Sometimes you have to be a lion, so you can be
the lamb you really are.
(Yvonne Seon, 2021)

Not all of the experiences the men I spoke to included the race or ethnicity of the people involved. However, I thought the meaning in the stories were too powerful not to tell. More often than not, these stories were about finding the silver lining during the twin-pandemic or, when unable to do this, recognizing that their mission was to trudge through the strife to inspire and to provide hope and space for the next generation.

Silver Linings

With COVID-19 restrictions making socializing more difficult and racial injustices adding an additional obstacle, Black men seemed to be assailed from all sides. However, while the effects of this were felt, so too was the ability to find moments of joy. For example, Izaak wished he could have had more human interaction to combat the loneliness he felt during COVID-19 isolation, "I miss human interaction enough to want to drive to work and waste my gas (laughs)." However he found other ways to get human interaction, and when he did, he made sure to appreciate it, "I can go to a restaurant or a bar [and] like once you sit down [and] get your fucking mask off (laughs), and you can like sit and have a drink and kind of just chill like it was normal."

Despite the difficulties, many spoke to moments of joy that resulted directly from seeing global outrage for the Black Americans murdered during the twin-pandemic and justice for the wrongs committed, as Izaak noted: "When [the] George Floyd case kinda went the world's way . . . [and Derek Chauvin] got the verdict you needed. [Matt: Yeah.] I think that that was one." Though trepidatious of being too hopeful, participants still embraced a cautious hope for change. The strength of a global, collective message provided comfort. Zahair commented, "Marches that are going nationwide and beyond the nation like worldwide. We had people marching in Korea we had marching in Japan, Australia, England, France, everywhere." For Oscar, this helped awaken his humanity, "I think what also helped was when I started seeing the protests . . . not just in America, but all over the world . . . that helped me man . . . to get me out of my school mind and, and put me back into being a human." Some found creative spaces to voice their opinions and connect with others, as Oscar told me:

> [The] few [White] people that I did talk to you about it, they were allies . . . [and] people hit me up because I was on Facebook blowing people up, blowing White people up. So, [then these] White people [said], Hey, can we talk about race? So . . . I started a group for teachers, I had got about fifty or sixty teachers talking about race. And this all happened because of what I said on Facebook. And most of these teachers were White or Hispanic.

Many described making space for community growth and action, and while they participated in and created their own protests, they additionally allowed themselves to savor the joy sparked by seeing the youth protest. Zahair, for instance, said, "I was kinda overjoyed . . . it was a multitude of races, and like young people . . . just marchin."

These men also created space to process things on their own. Atukwei noted that "going home was always my, my place of self-care, just escaping campus and turning off my phone." They also sought out communities that provided space for knowledge and resonance. For example, Atukwei talked to me about attending Zoom conference calls with high-ranking Black executives where they discussed their experiences of racism and triumph: "Honestly, that lit my joy up for people to be connecting their passions and wanted to see change even in the world that they lived in."

The Next Generation

The final subtheme references the next generation. There were multiple instances when Oscar and Niles, who were older than the other interviewees, expressed their desire for me to succeed. Oscar said, "I need you to win," and described his faith in the resilience and pursuits of the next generation to share the truth of the twin-pandemic, "People like yourself and others down the line are going to do research on COVID and how it impacted Black and Brown people . . . and they're already telling people about the disparities." They expressed a desire to see us all succeed, and in order to do that, demonstrated a commitment to support other Black men to the best of their ability. As Niles put it: "I have to figure out, are we maximizing each other . . . because you're getting ready to reach a[n] audience. . . . You're getting ready to hold a voice."

As a younger Black man, Zahair stated his positive emotional experience of participating in and seeing other people his age and younger participate in change through protest, "I was extremely happy that so many people actually came out, like so many young people that actually came out and actually, you know, took it seriously." Even though he was in a different phase of life than Oscar and Niles, he was able to set his ego aside for the betterment of everyone, "It's not even really about me. It's really about this generation and us you know, making sure that we know what the good fight is."

Interpretations and Synthesis

The men I spoke to would often try to find the positive in a difficult situation or find additional reserves of motivation by reminding themselves that they can and should inspire the next generation. Research has suggested a common response to adversity is trying to find a silver lining (Seery, 2011), often through cognitive reappraisal (Troy et al., 2010), which is essentially reframing a situation in your head to create a different, and better, meaning. The most common silver lining my interviewees mentioned was global protests. Participants were aware of their constant state of resilience, and while they wished their lives and the lives of other Black people could be easier, they appreciated seeing people from all over the world with different backgrounds and identities come together to protest the killing of Black Americans.

They would also use cognitive reappraisal by keeping the next generation in mind when we were discussing the difficulty of their own experiences. To me, this meant that they were willing to continue to put up suffering for the sake of others. Where problems may have been too daunting for them individually, they could find motivation in knowing that they are making the world better for Black people to come.

11

Learning From Past Generations

I think, I hope, that the objective reader, in following my life, the life of only one ghetto-created Negro, may gain a better picture and understanding than he has previously had . . . Thicker each year in these ghettoes is the kind of teenager that I was, with the wrong kinds of heroes, and the wrong kinds of influences.
(Malcolm X, 1965)

If I allow myself, I'll begin to drift. I'll drift into a space that bursts a silent cacophony of emotions: my mind. It's here where I find myself saddened, yet resolute, that the only clue to the observant fly on the wall into my experience is the water collecting slowly in my eyes as I write you this. You see, the emotional training I received at the intersection of my Black masculine identity whilst raised around White people still lingers with me. An almost indescribable urge I can best translate in the tone of a whisper: don't let them see you struggle. Why? Well, I'm Black. And what does that mean?

Well, for me Ms. Angela Bassett said it best, it's when you "have to work twice as hard in life to get half as far" (Ansari & Yang, 2017). In other words, there isn't time. While I cannot speak to her intersectional experience, I am thankful for her words. I wrote this so that what lay beneath my thick skin, which is necessary for every Black man, could have cathartic voice. My emotional vacillation, which I intentionally share, is my own work, and the writing of this, my intervention.

And so I drift into my emotions that give rise to thoughts. Together they create a holy blend of appreciation for those who have come before me. Without them, I would not be. Without them, I could not reach myself let alone you in this way, from a position of educational privilege and comfort in my identities. My mother and father, raised in poverty in Baltimore, Maryland, where would I be without you as both my shield and spear? The trials of your time and the ones before, where would I be if not for the actions that followed your triumphs and failures?

We are the footprint that follows the conclusion of our ancestor's journey's. Both separate from and a continuation of them, we are connected. Those before us yearn for our success, and this theme shined brightly as my interviewees took heed to the lessons of their elders. What came from our conversations illuminated the absorption of and appreciation for these lessons and strength from previous generations of Black people.

The men I spoke to often leveraged the obstacles previous generations faced to motivate them through current adversity, as when Oscar discussed family history, "I was starting to put all the research that I had done in life, [and] lessons that my dad taught me. My dad was the best thing." Oscar uses the experience of his father as armor to protect himself during the twin-pandemic:

> My dad survived Emmett Till, right. My dad, my dad was born on a plantation, you hear me? Plantation! . . . My dad didn't even have running water man. . . . I remember going to see my grandparents, and having to take a bath in a washtub and having to go outside and using an outhouse. . . . People have to realize when they would talk to me, and they want to tell me, [oh] the Civil War was [long] ago and Reconstruction was longer. They, they forget, they forget man, my people were around then, and I actually knew my people who were around then. (Laughs.) . . . My [great]-grandfather was born in [1869]. . . . Come on man, that was during Reconstruction. So, you know, these are my people.

Oscar comfortably paid homage to older Black folx, as did many of the other men. For instance, Niles discussed how he "glorifies" those who have come before him,

> I'm a person that understands our history and I'm big on celebrating and doing something about what they and our ancestors and people of the past have sacrificed, to think that we can be business owners or have degrees or write dissertations.

Niles additionally talked about a hardship he faced recently, and the power of the love shared between his father and himself,

> It was a couple days ago and [I] said dad, you know I was crying in his, in his arms. [Matt: Yeah.] I just said thank you, man, for not giving up on me. [Matt: Yeah.] Thank you for believing in me and thank you for encouraging me. Thank you for having time for me, and that's the joy that I speak to today.

Some men found an appreciation and interest in researching the history of Black community in an attempt to leverage it for themselves and others. Zahair provided an example of this by referencing an African proverb that helps him as a pacifist,

> There's a quote that says, "A child not loved by their village burns the village."[7] So, you know,

> even if they're Black people who I just don't agree with . . . I'd rather you still be my brother or my sister and disagree.

Additionally, while talking about the twin-pandemic, many of these Black men expressed appreciation for both the protection their parents provided while they were coming of age, and their parents' resilience. For example, after having the highest GPA in his predominantly White elementary school, Zahair recalled the heartbreak he had as he sat in his school's award ceremony and watched as his classmates were called to walk across stage and be presented for honor roll. However, Zahair never heard his name called. While acknowledging how painful it was for him, he also gave space, respect, and appreciation for the holistic experience of his mother, who had to go to his predominantly White school in the South to confront the situation,

> You know your parents are still their own human beings. I mean, I get like their duty is to take care of you . . . at the same time [they] still go to work, deal with their own racism at work. . . . I can imagine [it] to this day . . . [my mom] having like probably a terrible day that day, like her boss yelling at her or someone said something slick

---

[7] "A child that is not embraced by the village will burn it down to feel its warmth." (African proverb)

racist to her. Or she had to deal with some sexism at work or something like that . . . [then] come home to your kid crying, telling you, yeah, they didn't give me honor roll. So you've had a crappy day . . . then the next day you have to go to school . . . argue with them all day about why they did this to your kid or why is my kid being treated like this? . . . And it's because my kid's Black, but you can't ask that directly, because they're going to deny it. So you got to [ask] little questions and be like, what happened? And then they'd have no [excuse]. So then now she knows it's because my kid is Black. So now I have to let my kid deal with this for the two or three months [before] the next semester and then pull them out.

A heavy, complex weight was given to Zahair's mother. While experiencing the burden of the twin-pandemic, some of the Black men I interviewed shared stories of gratitude for how their parents tried to protect them from the cognitive and psychological burden of racism while still trying to make sure they were prepared. As Marcel explained to me,

> My mom didn't really expose that world to me. It was more so just like how you should live, and you know, your morals, stuff like that. But me and my brother, we were both like riding our

> bikes. And [were] in [town name]. And one time we went into like [a] cul-de-sac area. . . . It was like this older White man and his son on the porch, and it was the first time in my life like I had ever heard the word nigger. Like I had no idea. But I remember he like shouted at us and we were like ten and eleven at the time. I got scared . . . [he said,] "Get out of here niggers," and we just sped off and we went home and told my mom, and that was like one of the first times for sure where I guess like, my bubble, my personal bubble that I created was popped.. . . And I had the whole like real heart-to-heart talk [with my mom about how] people feel a certain way about us because of the color of our skin.

Actions of self-sacrifice and messages of relentless pursuit were the gifts given to most of these Black men by their parents, grandparents and ancestors. As Oscar explained, "If I, if I quiet, I'm letting down everybody on my ancestors. . . . So I gotta, I gotta stand up for our people man because if we don't stand up, Nobody else will." Though some of these messages were complex: "You're telling a ten-year-old kid to be good, but not too good . . . be better than them, but not too better" (Zahair), these Black men were nonetheless appreciative. Keen to the wisdom and care embedded in their parents' messages, they see a clearer vision of America for

Black men that they used to traverse not only the twin-pandemic but also life before and after. Zahair explained:

> Looking back now, I get what they're trying to say . . . because if you underperform, they're gonna be like, oh look at him he's Black, of course he's underperforming, like duh. And then like if you overperform it's like, Oh . . . you know, they only give him a pass because he is Black.

***

Interpretations and Synthesis

As I walked through life during the twin-pandemic, I recognized just how much I was able to leverage stories from my parents, extended family, and ancestors to understand the current problems in the world around me. This is a phenomenon perhaps most notably recognized in slave narratives (Barret, 1995) and stories and songs passed down from generations. The act of "counter storytelling," the second tenet of CRT, spoke to my own experience and that of others. Resisting the dominant narrative with our own stories, arming ourselves with the experiences of family members and other same-race peers, created a heuristic system of safety.

The majority of the interviewees did not connect previous generations' experiences to their own way of navigating the world when I asked directly, "Growing up, what stories were you told about our criminal justice system and medical system? In what ways did you use these stories to navigate the last year?" However, when answering other questions most of these men did provide stories from their parents or previous generations and explained how they utilized these stories to understand the world. It was an interesting, yet clear dynamic that told me while they could not conjure up examples when asked directly, they could and often would pull stories from their memory to respond to adversity. From where I sat, it felt like one degree of separation from an instinct. A skill they were so familiar with they sometimes forgot they even had it.

12

Implications and Directions

Bhikkhus, the teaching is merely a vehicle to
describe the truth.
Don't mistake it for the truth itself. A finger
pointing at the moon is not the moon.
The finger is needed to know where to look for
the moon, but if you mistake the finger for the
moon itself, you will never know the real moon.
(Thich Nhat Hanh)

I'll be honest, I'm new to this field as a professional. And because of this I feel a palpable fear extend from my heart to my hand that is attempting to reach out and connect with other members in my field, especially those whose tenure is supported by many trips around the sun. I'm afraid I cannot provide the well-rounded assessment you'd like. However, I find it necessary to continue not in spite of this, but because of it. While I acknowledge that I have much to learn, as we all do, I believe I have much to give as well. So as a new member of the field, but a man who possesses the skin tone you've asked to hear from (Akbar & Parker, 2021) and whose racial kin have long been impacted by access to health care and mental health resources, it is important that I do not hold back my opinion. My hope, with attempted humility, is to emulate the importance and need to challenge the systems we are part of, regardless of the fields we are in. I would like to use this chapter to especially challenge those in the fields of helping and healing.

It behooves our work as active allies and or clinicians to stay up-to-date on current social issues, and, if we are being honest with ourselves, we as a society have been bombarded with many over the past few years (Kreiger, 2020). Many scholars answered the call to action and engaged in research focused on mental health impacts related to the COVID-19 pandemic (Castelnuovo et al., 2021; Riehm et al., 2021). However, not as many have incorporated positive functioning in their definition of mental health. Further, despite Black Americans being placed under a microscope from 2020 to 2022 and having a uniquely difficult experience during COVID-19 (Bowleg, 2020), a dearth of research has looked at their experiences of mental health in a context of recent racial traumas and social injustices. It is important we do so, and that we do so by hearing directly from them in an effort to actively incorporate their narratives. This book is the first study, to my knowledge, examining the experiences of Black men at the intersection of COVID-19 and social injustice using narrative analysis and CRT to articulate their holistic experiences of resilience and well-being.

The inclusion of culture in the therapy room has become more common over the last few decades (Atkinson et al., 1998). Additionally, since 2017 the guidelines of the American Psychological Association have encouraged multiculturalism (American Psychological Association, 2017). I would go so far as to say that doing so is necessary for ethically minded clinical work. It is important for us as clinicians to ask ourselves and our systems if we are doing everything we can to understand and work effectively with clients from different races. The key word here is *doing*. There is a significant difference between being aware of multiculturalism—what is often called "cultural competence"—and using it in the therapy room or with colleagues—often known as cultural sensitivity (D'Aniello et al., 2016). This research speaks to the importance of clinicians' active approach to undoing social injustice. Social psychologists have even shown that clients sometimes experience negative affect, decreased attention, and decreased cognitive capacity during interracial therapeutic relationships (Jordan et al., 2012). One reason for this may be that Black participants often spend cognitive energy considering if interracial interactions would become racially insensitive interactions. This aligns with statements from Black men in this study who held reservations about engaging in critical race dialogues with White peers out of a fear that those White peers would display racial insensitivities.

In line with previous scholars' work in our field (Falicov, 2014), I propose that it is our job as therapists to *set the table* regarding topics of sociopolitical identity and how they relate to power and privilege. In the therapy room, not only are we in a position of power, but our actions or lack of actions impact the transmission of power in the therapy room and in our clients' worlds (Ward, 2012). As we think about the current climate of sociocultural identity and recent atrocities, it is incumbent that we make known that conversations about power, privilege, oppression, and identity can be had. Explicitly acknowledging current events and the intersection of those events with our own identities may unburden the minds of Black male clients (and others) who may be unsure if topics of racism can be given credence and discussed. I invite you as current or future professionals to consider the roles you hold (teacher, mentor, student, researcher, therapist, etc.) and how you can learn more to *do* more.

Our work extends far beyond the four walls of therapy. When I was in my master's program, I recall attending my required supervision with a doctoral-level clinician in an affluent town. Feeling full of rage after my third irritating interaction with police in the town, I shared with the clinician my exhaustion and anger toward the police system, explaining that they would just as quickly pull me over if they thought I was doing something wrong as disregard me when I needed help. In response to my frustration, my supervisor explained that the police sometimes pull over Black people because they think the Black people are in the town to steal cars. The clinician then provided me with this recommendation: "Next time, just tell them you're here to see me." This story, now more than half a decade old, hangs with me. This individual did not see how their actions indirectly perpetuated racism; further, they did not recognize the power they had to work against this. We as professionals need to find creative ways to become immersed in policy and community reform. As some of the most educated in our communities, it is not enough to provide myopic solutions to the "isms" that currently plague our society. We have no excuse for failing to use our power and privilege of education to challenge the things we know to be wrong. These officers believed I was a criminal—another n-word from Newark here to disrupt their peaceful society—and my supervisor thought compassion was to give me what felt like a voucher that allowed me to be in their town. Indirectly buying into the narrative of Black males as problematic still purchases the item, and I do not need nor do I want you to increase its stock. While today I hold no anger toward this individual, we need to do better. The men in this book have highlighted how marginalized communities have already developed strategies to endure immediate and systemic wrongdoings. Those of us in the fields of helping and healing should direct our energy and compassion toward learning about and subsequently challenging and undoing systems of oppression.

In a world of racial wounds there is much healing to be done (Hardy, 2013). It is important that therapists of color engage in their own process of healing from racial trauma and that White therapists become active allies. While we as clinicians, researchers, and academics have in recent years done better at inviting conversations about race, those conversations have often been heavily sterilized by intellectualization and projection. With specific reference to White allyship, I fear many White people seeking to be allies have instead tried to actively remove themselves from the room in this way. Rather than delving into conversation that incorporates and processes their own experiences and biases, they have flaunted a racial consciousness (Foste, 2020). It is important we recognize that this approach hurts us all and that we instead challenge ourselves and others to grow.

Future Directions

Little effort has ever been dedicated to understanding Black male experiences. And if I'm keeping it real, the minimal work that does exist often irritates me. This is because the archetype of Black men, even at the highest levels of academic conversation, remains enthralled with the idea that we have a developmental or psychological desire to *be the White man.* Whether you consider this to be an indictment of this idea or not, I candidly don't care. However, I do ask that you try to fully understand me. My words are not here to say that the phenomenon of internalized Black hatred does not exist. Rather, I'd like us all to question why we are so fixated on it. What is it about our society that makes us immediately use White men as a barometer of normalcy? Just as a Black man's pursuit of white skin gets him further from liberation, so too does our obsession with this idea. Focusing on desired whiteness still centralizes whiteness. It still perpetuates a dynamic of white supremacy by stating, "Yes, of course they must want to be like us." Can you see how this is both myopic and offensive? Hard pass.

Instead, what if we adjusted our vision and focused on the basic human respect and personhood given to White men? Can we as a country cut through the delusion of desiring whiteness and see the truth in the stories of the oppressed, who tell us: We desire dignity and freedom. I do not want to be you; I want to be me. Yet the path to this is not always clear. So much like Tommy J. Curry in his book *The Man-Not*, I yearn for Black male studies not only for myself, but for others as well.

Speaking of others . . . One of the most difficult challenges I faced in doing this study was thinking about other identities affected by social injustice yet not being able to fully include their experiences here. Through this process I have often thought about my Black sisters, my Asian and Latin American family, and all BIPOC folx that have also had to endure. If you hold these identities, I would like you to know that while I did not have the capacity to open this study to everyone who may have needed it, my hope is this research will inspire or give academic credibility for other researchers, perhaps even you, to explore the experiences of other groups. It is imperative that our field acknowledge and analyze the direct experience of those who have had to endure through twin-pandemics. This necessity is also a prime opportunity for us to pull apart our harmful systems—including policing, government, and education—and learn to rebuild them.

13

Unapologetically Yours,

Can you walk with me?
I hope we'll find the reason why
we often sob, go on cry
Painful memories f—— up the vibe
Though I be tryna let the time heal my mind
I was once a child, I've gotten older
Still, I know I'm just a boy in God's eyes
Fill me up with wisdom and some courage
Plus endurance to survive, help mine thrive
(Jermaine Cole, 2020)

After days of feeling stuck with how and where to begin this final chapter, I recognized how immersed I was—and in some ways still am—in my own head. Candidly, there was a part of me that hoped in doing this book, I would find some sort of answer. I don't have an answer; however, what I do have are the lessons of previous mentors, and my practice rooted in Zen, reverberating in my mind, telling me to get out of my head and into my heart. This section is my attempt to do just that. Frankly, whether you feel subjected to, enthralled in, or a lingering indifference towards the idea, this is my book, a part of my healing, and I stake my claim in this chapter to discuss where my heart is.

I find myself tired, I find myself scared. From 2020 to 2022, I've spent special focus and energy trying to listen to the sounds of the world from my same-race peers, as well as those who hold different racial and ethnic identities and different socio-political or political beliefs. In order to write this book authentically, I believed it was necessary to do this. However, I notice a part of myself that is upset. This feeling comes from a disappointment in what has felt like many people's lack of curiosity and unwillingness to listen to the opinions of others. Specifically, I'd like to point to the construct of whiteness that was created and still exists since the seventeenth century (Menakem, 2017), and those White people who, knowingly or otherwise, have absorbed the poisonous ideals. In my short time on this earth, these last few years have displayed for me, clearer than ever, an expectation of those with privileged racial identities that their voices will be heard. I will not take from anybody the right to be heard, and, at least on paper, neither does our Constitution. However, to me it has felt like that expectation has led to more expectation. In that those with privilege have been experienced, by me, as having an entitled disposition that with any utterance, their every desire should be met and that an inability or unwillingness to meet these demands is perceived as some sort of infringement on their humanity.

Though I find momentary solace in the sagacity of words that shed light on to this, "when you're accustomed to privilege, equality feels like oppression," it's fleeting. I asked myself what I want from White people who live in a world of systemic acceptance, where it feels, from outsider perspective, your sole obstacle in America, if at all, is to find your ticket marked "grit," and barriers rotate like turnstiles. Where my experience tells me that those who hold skin color like mine must do more. I'm upset at all the White people who over these past few years have shared with me their moments of enlightened disappointment in our systems, such as how they "just can't trust the government anymore." I notice myself look at them from within my empathic mask. For a while, this was the only guard that hid the listless eyes that play the systemic abuse experienced by my ancestors, grandparents, parents, and me on a loop in my head. I want to ask how you've gone so long with such faith, and at the same time a White friend of mine told me, "You know, this might be the first pandemic for a lot of White people." But we've been here. For centuries we have been in a pandemic; you've only just noticed. This system, as some of my interviewees alluded to, was built for you. I do not have the time to bring us further from truth with the placation of your emotions. Moreover, though it is often scary for me, it is because I care very much for you, my country, and myself that I refuse to play disingenuous games. With time, and ill will, the weed of whiteness is far too meticulously and deeply rooted for us to pluck at stems and believe it to be gone.

"I Don't Have a Dog in This Fight"

I'd like to move the barometer to the idea of moderation which many people flirted with before, during, and no doubt after the twin pandemic. Finding a genuine place of moderation in life is often difficult and involves a great deal of work. As humans we all have biases, preferences, and tendencies that constantly pull us in certain directions. Discovering moderation, in a general sense, is finding acceptance and balance. When done well, moderation is a great strength that sees all sides of a problem, and consequently encourages others to consider doing the same before embarking off in a particular direction. In this way everyone may experience validation and come closer together. However—and let me be direct—moderation in the presence of oppression is unacceptable. For those who find themselves here, I notice I am fearful of you, yet I am also tethered to you. I find myself quietly frightened by your moderation because I don't know your next move. However, I recognize, as a result of understanding history, what happens in your stagnation. As Dr. King explained to White church leaders in Birmingham,

> First, I must confess that over the past few years I have been gravely disappointed with the

> white moderate. I have almost reached the regrettable conclusion that the Negro's great stumbling block in his stride toward freedom is not the White Citizen's Council-er or the Ku Klux Klanner, but the white moderate, who is more devoted to "order" than to justice; who prefers a negative peace which is the absence of tension to a positive peace which is the presence of justice; who constantly says: "I agree with you in the goal you seek, but I cannot agree with your methods of direct action"; who paternalistically believes he can set the timetable for another man's freedom; who lives by a mythical concept of time and who constantly advises the Negro to wait for a "more convenient season." Shallow understanding from people of good will is more frustrating than absolute misunderstanding from people of ill will. Lukewarm acceptance is much more bewildering than outright rejection. (King, 1963)

Though I'm afraid, at this point I cannot relent because I need to dig deeper into what I believe is a case of mistaken identity. What we have come to see is a phenomenon in which many who actually hold indifference have mistaken their identity as a moderate. As I alluded to above, moderate is a distinction to be earned. It is to say in this context that I have listened to the sounds of the world, I have read the words of Baldwin, King, and Pac. I have connected their words to the contemporary stories of Kendi, Bryan Stevenson, and Kendrick, who artistically weave the continued history of racial trauma from current events into their work. Moderation is a proclamation that you've just as diligently sought the words of William F. Buckley Jr., Thomas Sowell, and their ideological kin who covered Fox News during this time and somehow come to a conclusion that there exists a space between these metaphorical aisles that holds validity; that allows for liberation. I call this indifference because you and I both know you've had the time. I imagine your education, like mine, lacked a clear analysis of racial trauma. However, if you expect me to believe you have not heard the cries, my face will remain unshaken. I know you've seen our world tell us to stand up all while their boot lays firmly on our chests. Where were you? It is my belief that you feign moderation but at your core use what is actually indifference as a means of self-preservation. You'd rather avoid the uncomfortable conversation—because you can—than ruffle feathers. All at the cost of another life. It is this very dynamic that points us back to the beginning. There is no moderation when oppression is on one side of the spectrum. And so, I say this with as much love as I can muster, get over yourself.

I want to believe that you mean no harm, because in private spaces I find love and acceptance from you; at the same time, when called upon in big moments it feels like you shrink. In your attempt to do no harm by not engaging, you allow harm to be done. And if you, from wherever you are now, say, "No, I am well versed in these topics, and I truly believe in a stance of moderation," I do not feel safe around you. If you are truly moderate, I'm sure this makes sense to you. I have no doubt we have much to talk about, but it may be from a distance.

Lastly, I want to address why you may have come here. Looking for answers, perhaps? If so, I invite you to reflect on that. When you picked up this book by a Black author, ask yourself, was there part of you that wanted me to give you answers on how to engage in situations? Did you come here looking for a step-by-step guide on how to avoid being seen as racist? If so, you've already made your first mistake. While I appreciate your desire to do better, I have no interest in living up to the dynamic of white infallibility that is seething in our culture to this day. I have no interest in providing you a checklist to save you from making mistakes, because they will happen. I have no interest in putting words to paper that help you find excuses for what went wrong after you followed the guide to the letter and things didn't work out your way. Too often we use these scripts as an excuse, as a way to say "I tried" and it didn't work, so now I'm not going to try any more.

For centuries we have used stories to point to experiences—religious and spiritual experiences, as well as everyday interactions. In many ways this book came into being because of spiritual teachings. Such teachings, when understood correctly, guide us, and so too does this book try its best to point you to the moon. Please do not get so wrapped up in it that you miss the moons. What are the moons? The moons are the people in your life. Like a child looking up at the night sky for the first time humbled with unbridled curiosity, we too must become again as a child[8] to see the truth of the moon's beauty. The experiences that created its craters and the innate ability to shine even when darkness surrounds it. Each day, it is up to you to continue in your humility and curiosity to learn how to respond. If you find yourself in opposition to these statements or unsure about where to go next, perhaps take a moment to go nowhere. Perhaps you should sit and allow these ideas and experiences to be considered valid for what they are, and, if you feel so brave, allow yourself to play with them in careful curiosity.

Family

While in my experience it's felt like some White people have tried to eject entirely from this reality, I must also recognize those White allies with muddied shovels who have actively tried to listen, engage, and challenge themselves and our systems with new ideas that adjust our culture's way of thinking and way of life. Who over these last few years have

---

[8] Matthew 18:3: "Unless you are converted and become like children you will never enter the kingdom of heaven." Note: I do not interpret this passage from the Christian Bible to mean that you should convert to being Christian; rather, I believe it calls us to convert to being connected to all things.

considered new perspectives about the entrenched structures that are working against people who look like me. Who have the humility and moxie to realize the ways they themselves have absorbed these harmful practices. To these White allies I say: I need you. I need you to continue to walk with us by courageously enacting what you know to be right in spaces that find creative ways to do wrong.

To my Black folx and BIPOC allies: Many philosophers, mystics, and religious texts talk about adversity as a constant part of life. As the Buddha said, "Life is duhkha [suffering]."[9] If it has felt like individuals or groups have weaponized this claim as a means to obfuscate the suffering you and those before you have endured—ex. "we all have problems, get over it"—I write you this to let you know that you are not alone. These words have hurt you, as they have me. I've had to lean heavily on my meditative practice to find compassion toward people who hold these ideologies, despite feeling the conditions required of me to have worth in their eyes only increasing. I find myself wishing I had an answer for you to save you from suffering. However, I recognize this desire as a compassionate grandiosity. So please allow me to try to humble myself. I do not know what this book will mean to you, and I will not venture to guess. I hope you allow it to mean whatever it means to you. The men whose voices you have heard in this book, myself included, have

---

[9] In Buddhism, duhkha is the first of the Four Noble Truths.

before and after this twin-pandemic accepted the double-bind experience of our adversity, regardless of societal acceptance, and done our best to find our identities and make them functional.

I was reading the ancient Hindu text, *The Bhagavad Gita*, and thought of you. In it we are shown two paths pure of heart: Jnana yoga, the contemplative path of wisdom, and karma yoga, the path of selfless action (Easwaran, 2007). With both leading us in the same direction, it is not about which is right or wrong, but rather which is true to the individual. I hope you are able to find your path that leads you closer to healing, validation, and understanding. As a therapist, teacher, researcher, scholar, advocate, ally, Black man, son, brother, or any other identity I can enumerate, they all lead back to the same root. I am undeniably human, like you who read this; we are from the same soil. Though I know very little, my many hats have taught me many things, and one is to lean into discomfort. If you've made it this far, I thank you for doing the same, and also would like to remind you that, no matter how far you have come, this is only the beginning. I hope we both maintain our curiosity and humility. Dae ja dae bi, Matt.

I been scared and battered.
My hopes the wind done scattered.
Snow has friz me,
Sun has baked me,
Looks like between 'em they done
Tried to make me
Stop laughin', stop lovin', stop livin'—
But I don't care!
I'm still here!
(Hughes, 1957)

FULL METHODS

With the first global pandemic in over a century, the world experienced unique problems which were new to our generation, and disproportionately impacted marginalized communities, particularly Black men. Simultaneously, experiences of social injustice did not cease for Black men in the United States. This created a novel experience where in the midst of the COVID-19 health pandemic, Black men were also victims and witnesses to multiple social injustices and unequal justice systems in comparison to their White peers. At the time this study was conducted, little research had explored experiences of Black men during the pandemic. Further, research had yet to examine the impact of the twin pandemic on Black men in a qualitative fashion while also considering resilience and well-being.

The purpose of this study was to understand obstacles Black cisgender men faced while contending with the twin pandemic, while simultaneously noting potential effects on their well-being and highlighting ways Black men utilized resilience. Further, connecting these findings to CRT would be additionally novel and help provide future research with a deeper understanding and paradigm to consider. This section is intended to thoroughly articulate the methodology of the research shared in this book, including theoretical foundation, research development/design, participant selection, demographics, interview processes, assimilation/analysis of data, and researcher considerations, specifically my and the audit team's backgrounds and positions related to the present topic.

Theoretical Basis of the Methodology

Utilizing narrative analysis, this study attempted to capture, as best it could, the stories of social injustice, resilience, and well-being in Black cisgender men who lived in the United States during the *twin pandemic*: the global COVID-19 pandemic, as well as globally-broadcast injustices against their same-race peers, in addition to personal experiences of racism. Additionally, this study reflected on the participants' stories by drawing connections to Critical Race Theory (CRT) in an effort to create further clarity and understanding for future research and conversation. In semi-structured interviews with six Black men I explored the following questions:

Research Question and Major Questions

1. What was the last year like for Black men surviving the twin pandemic?
    a. Major Q1: How did Black men show resilience through the past year in regard to

managing the twin pandemic (COVID-19 and social injustice)?

b. Major Q2: In what ways did Black men experience their well-being during the twin pandemic?
c. Major Q3: In what ways did Black men's interpersonal relationships (e.g., family, friends, and community) play a role in their own resilience/well-being and resilience/well-being of others?
d. Major Q4: Did Black men show learned resilience strategies from previous generations or their community (e.g., mothers, fathers, and grandparents) in handling their problems over the last year?

Narrative Analysis

Narrative inquiry was selected because it encourages action, group mobilization, and sense of belonging (Riessman, 2008). People are storytellers (Frank, 2010) and narrative analysis is a collection of qualitative methods, which intends to make sense of these stories. The purpose for using narrative analysis was to capture the stories of those interviewed, instead of how society reflects their narrative to the larger masses. Seminal research would also suggest that the most informative material generated through qualitative interviews are the stories told in the interviews (Mishler,

1986). With the United States' poor history of creating and reflecting deleterious narratives of Black Americans, it is especially important to keep the power in the hands of the storytellers. Moreover, narrative methodology intends to highlight the connection between the individuals and their cultural context (Bloomberg & Volpe, 2019). Additionally, the present study analyzed and synthesized results using thematic analysis (Braun & Clarke, 2014; Riessman, 2008), which placed emphasis on the themes being articulated by the participants and their connection to pre-existing factors (e.g., research questions).

Critical Race Theory

Including CRT as a paradigm was intentional, not only because it blends harmoniously with narrative methodology—as its intent is to educate and translate informative discourse through narratives—but because CRT was also established through racially charged moments in the United States, such as *Brown v. Board of Education of Topeka* and the Civil Rights Movement of the 1960s (Delgado & Stefancic, 2017; Tate IV, 1997). Because this study looked to give voice to Black men's reactions to contemporary (March 2020-March 2022) socio-political/politically-charged events through their stories, it served the study well to incorporate a paradigm that blends well to narratives.

Born from the field of law, CRT, according to Delgado and Stefancic (2017), intends to look critically at social, legal, and economic systems through five tenets: (1) racism is ordinary and not aberrational; (2) interest convergence; (3) social construction; (4) storytelling and counter storytelling; and (5) structural determinism. See Chapter 4 for descriptions of each tenet.

Participants and Data Collection

Narrative analysis can include various participant narratives, while looking at how participants assign meaning to their stories, themes between the narratives, and how they address the research questions or go beyond the questions (Bloomberg & Volpe, 2019). Data for the current study explored six participants who identified as cisgender Black men (African American), and resided in the United States between March 13, 2020, and March 13, 2022. To open itself to diverse narrative experiences across life phases, participant ages could range from 21 and 65. Because acts of violence and responses to COVID-19 varied across the country, I recruited participants from geographically diverse regions within the United States.

Following approval from the University of Kansas Institutional Review Board, participants were selected through snowball sampling, utilizing emailing from personal and professional contacts. Personal and professional contacts were asked to forward a statement of recruitment in the present study to Black men who met the inclusion criteria. Referred participants were then asked to review and fill out preliminary information via a Qualtrics survey, which included the purpose of the study with a statement of consent, and a brief demographic questionnaire. All participants met inclusion criteria and interviews were scheduled via email or cell phone, and conducted virtually on Zoom between February and March 2022.

Utilizing the openness of the cultural formulation interview (American Psychiatric Association, 2013) I was able to have a fluid, semi-structured interview foundation. In the consideration of the development of interview questions, I sought to pass power to participants in the creation of their own theory through their narratives, emphasizing emancipation of their experience rather than control (Georges, 2005). Interview questions were then created out of an amalgamative process with consideration of narrative inquiry's intent to harness the power of stories (Riessman, 2008) by asking about specific events in time as well as CRT's importance of stories (counter narratives) and its premise that racism is not an aberration. However, I also recognize the limitation of my own experience and imagination to capture everyone's experience. To allow for openness of participant narratives, salient narratives that do not fit within these phenomena were also provided consideration to be included depending on if they connected to themes across participants. In short, if other people mentioned it, it was included.

Interviews were approximately 45–60 minutes in length with eleven potential semi-structured questions and room for follow-up questions. All items were pre-screened through expert opinions of Black men living in the United States. Additionally, to ensure clarity and fluidity of items, as well as interview processes, the items were piloted prior to the study by a volunteer who met criteria. In line with narrative analysis, questions were designed to allow for storied responses about race/racism, resilience, and well-being (Gubrium & Holstein, 1997). Further, questions were designed to have participants focus on or recall specific instances in time (Gubrium & Holstein, 1997; Riessman, 2008) to promote conversation that stays on topic.

The semi-structured interview consisted of the following questions/prompts:

1. Tell me a story about a time when you felt the impact of both the COVID-19 pandemic and the social injustice pandemic as a Black man. How did you take care of yourself?
2. Talk to me about conversations you've had with other Black men about the George Floyd murder? In what ways do you feel like these conversations impacted you?
3. Black deaths sparked BLM protests over the summer. Talk to me about what it was like having conversations with White friends or coworkers. Black friends or coworkers?

4. January 6th, 2021. Talk to me about what it was like having conversations with White friends or coworkers. Black friends or coworkers?
5. Growing up, what stories were you told about our criminal justice system and medical system? In what ways did you use these stories to navigate the last year?
6. Tell me a story from your life this past year that you feel really embodies what it is to be a Black man in America.
7. What events during the twin pandemic stand out most for you? Talk to me about why they stand out for you, and who you were able to talk to about it.
8. Tell me a story about a time during the twin pandemic when you felt connected to others.
9. If you could change one thing this past year about your everyday life, what would it be?
10. Earlier I asked you about experiences of difficulty during the twin pandemic. Did you notice ever experiencing joy? If so, tell me a tale about a moment of joy during the twin pandemic. If not, talk to me about your survival.
11. Did I miss anything?

Data Analysis

It behooved the study to collect multiple stories from Black men who experienced the twin pandemic to allow for a scaffolding towards a general theory, which one story, in its singularity, would not be able to provide (Bloomberg & Volpe, 2019; Brinkmann, 2014). To provide substantive grounding in theory, while also emphasizing story integrity, and developing themes that seek to answer the research questions (Bloomberg & Volpe, 2019; Riessman, 2008), this study used an open coding approach.

The process I used in breaking down and understanding the data loosely followed Bloomberg's (2007, as cited in Bloomberg & Volpe, 2019, p. 236) *Road Map for the Process of Qualitative Data Analysis: An Outline.* After completing all interviews independently, I uploaded the recorded Zoom video using Media Hub and their transcription function. To familiarize myself with the data, I personally completed a transcription check for each participant video while concurrently listing my potential biases. I coded transcripts using open coding method to minimize chances for my own potential biases and maximize story integrity, while developing themes that connected to the research questions (Bloomberg & Volpe, 2019; Riessman, 2008). This was done by coding with participant summarization instead of interpretation (i.e., analytic memos).

Codes were given colors that corresponded with their respective analytic memos. For example, for Participant 1, the code "must respond quick to adversity" was given the color light blue. Analytic memos (summaries of his statements) that referred to this code were highlighted light blue in his transcript (e.g., "When dealt a bad hand, we need to find a way to move forward regardless"). After all participant transcripts were coded, I connected each participant's respective codes to a major question it provided insight towards, if any. From here, I refamiliarized myself with the codes from each participant's transcript to create themes across all participants for each major question. Themes were limited to being referenced in one major question. Next, I created an example list of participants' statements for each major question to allow for more accurate reporting of participant findings. However, because qualitative research findings should remain fluid throughout the process (Bloomberg & Volpe, 2019), I continued to allow for the transition of codes and themes as new meaning was discovered.

Audit Team

My audit team was presented with my summaries of the transcripts and themes as they relate to the research questions. They were asked to assess if my summarizations were plausible for each participant prior to disseminating member checks. My audit team consisted of two colleagues: the first was a 27-year-old heterosexual Black American man from the "South" and from working class; the second was a Middle Eastern male from the "West Coast" and from middle class, who was experienced in literature on masculinity. Auditors suggested minor revisions, and upon completion of their audit, I sent the subsequent findings out to participants for member checks. I received minimal revisions from member checks.

Researcher as an Instrument and Researcher Biases

According to Creswell (2013), the researchers are a primary instrument for the research from construction, interviewing, data collection, coding, and interpretation. As principal researcher on the team, I find it necessary to briefly state my identities and position because the participants' lives, and my own life will serve to create a culminating narrative (Andrews et al., 2013; Bloomberg & Volpe, 2019).

I am a Black, cisgender male, raised in a middle-class home. My parents are both Black Americans who were born and raised in poverty in Baltimore, Maryland. My own upbringing took place in Pennsylvania near the metropolitan area of Philadelphia. However, my direct environment was suburban, largely surrounded by a predominantly White population including my primary and secondary schooling. I completed this study while I was a PhD Candidate in Counseling Psychology at the University of Kansas and had previously completed my master's degree in Marriage and Family Therapy in New Jersey. Race and racism have been a topic of discussion in my family of origin (FOO) and have been integral to my training as a clinician at both the master's and doctoral level.

It was common in my home to hear and learn from my father and mother's stories of daily racist experiences. It was easy to feel how these experiences impacted their lives, and they prioritized passing these stories down to my brothers and me to keep us safe. For example, I can recall my father teaching us how to avoid any and all police interactions because if we didn't, they would "throw the book at you." No doubt this was connected to his experiences with law enforcement growing up.

I, in part, developed the present topic after experiencing my own difficulties and frustrations with racism over the last year while contending with the twin pandemic. It felt like the world slowed down over the last few years (2020–2022) and Black Americans were in the thick of things, not only trying to survive a global health pandemic and the many forms of discrimination connected to that, but also seeing their same race peers continually on the news murdered and their experiences of discrimination doubted on the highest levels. Trying to find resiliency through these difficulties, while also feeling as though I needed to continually find ways to creatively resist the negative narratives being placed on me and my same race peers was difficult and took negative effects on my mental and physical well-being. However, rising up felt like an imperative, and in some ways a habit. This brought me again to the concept of resilience, specifically how I learned to be resilient and in what ways I have used resiliency. I did not think I was unique in this regard and wanted to use this study as a means to give voice to a few, who may represent the many.

Validation of Research

To promote research transparency, accuracy and soundness, this study utilized three domains of qualitative research validation: *trustworthiness, credibility, and transferability* (Bloomberg & Volpe, 2019; Lincoln & Guba, 1986; Vaillancourt, 2006).

In terms of **trustworthiness**, which is akin to quantitative understanding of internal and external validity, research procedures were uniform across participants (Lincoln & Guba, 1986; Vaillancourt, 2006). This included completing prescreening measures and pre-established questions for the interviews. These questions were pre-screened by experts in the field to ensure the questions covered the necessary content and holistic construct being studied. A limitation to trustworthiness, which is inherent to qualitative interviews are the length at which the interview will be conducted. I planned for each interview to be between 45–60 minutes; however, in the interest of balancing research authenticity and control with client narratives, exactness of the interview timeframe varied slightly between participants, but remained within the given time frame. A second limitation to the study was the ability for follow up questions. Narrative analysis emphasizes participants' stories and as a result, participant responses may prompt different follow up questions from the interviewer. While it can be considered that these are limitations to the study, they can also be considered strengths of the study as they illuminated more genuine conversation. It was because of the latter I elected to have this flexibility with my research.

To promote **credibility** of participant narratives, which refers to the accuracy of the accounts given by the participants (Patton, 2001), member checks were utilized (i.e., participant narratives were given back to each respective participant). Because much of the data recorded in narrative analysis is in the participants' own words, it was essential for the participants to have the ability to review reflections and summarizations made by the audit team and me regarding their respective accounts. Lastly, as principal researcher, I clearly explicate my own attitudes, biases, and identities to display transparency.

The last consideration for validation is **transferability**, which refers to the ability for the information to be generalized to existing literature and society (Bloomberg & Volpe, 2019). As previously noted, to assess for transferability it was essential to clearly explicate participant demographic information, the procedures and questions asked and my subjective positionality, so as to prevent potentially inaccurate interpretation of the results. This will also allow for recreation of the study. Secondly, to assist in transferability of research findings to existing discourses, the study utilized CRT as a reflective paradigm. CRT has been a widely accepted concept within psychology, education, and law (Delgado & Steffancic, 2016) and as such, provided substantial foundation for the extrapolation of research findings to the broader topic of race, racism and social injustice within varying fields of study.

References

"Henrietta Lacks": A Donor's Immortal Legacy. (2020). NPR. https: //www.npr.org/2010/02/02/123232331/henrietta-lacks-a-donors-immortal-legacy

Abdelfatah, R. (2020, June). *American Police.* NPR. https: //www.npr.org/transcripts/869046127

About the USPHS Syphilis Study | Tuskegee University. (2021). Tuskegee University. https: //www.tuskegee.edu/about-us/centers-of-excellence/bioethics-center/about-the-usphs-syphilis-study

Addis, M. E., & James R. Mahalik, J. R. "Men, masculinity, and the contexts of help seeking." *American psychologist* 58.1 (2003): 5.

AGBA, Michael Sunday; AGBA, A. M. Ogaboh; Chukwurah, Daniel Chi Jr. COVID-19 pandemic and workplace adjustments/ decentralization: a focus on teleworking in the new normal. Broad research in artificial intelligence and neuroscience. Available at: <https: //brain.edusoft.ro/index.php/brain/article/view/1080>. Date accessed: 30 Mar. 2022.https://choice.npr.org/index.html?origin=https://www.npr.org/transcripts/869046127

Akbar, M., & Parker, T. L. (2021). *Equity, diversity, and inclusion framework. American Psychological Association. 1-16.* https: //www.apa.org/about/apa/equity-diversity-inclusion/framework.pdf

Akbar, N. (1996). *Breaking the chains of psychological slavery.* Tallahassee, FL: Mind Productions Associates.

Aldous, C. R. (2005). Creativity in problem solving: Uncovering the origin of new ideas. *International Education Journal, 5*(5), 43–56.

Alexander, M. (2010). *The new jim crow: Mass incarceration in the age of colorblindness.* The New Press.

AlHumaid, J., Ali, S., & Farooq, I. (2020). The psychological effects of the COVID-19 pandemic and coping with them in saudi arabia. *Psychological Trauma: Theory, Research, Practice, and Policy, 12*(5), 505–7. http: // doi: dx.doi.org/10.1037/tra0000623

Allen, A. (2010). *Origins of the dred scott case: Jacksonian jurisprudence and the supreme court, 1837–1857.* Athens, GA: University of Georgia Press.

American Psychiatric Association. (2013). *Diagnostic and statistical manual of mental disorders* (5th ed.). https: //doi-org.ezproxy.frederick.edu/10.1176/appi.books.9780890425596

American Psychological Association. (2017). *Multicultural guidelines: An ecological approach to context, identity, and intersectionality.* Retrieved from: http: //www.apa.org/about/policy/multicultural-guidelines.pdf

American Psychological Association. (2021). *Advocacy.* https: //www.apa.org/advocacy/civil-rights/diversity

Anderson, A., & Melo, H. (2016). Neurogenetics of resilience. *The Oxford Handbook of Positive Psychology, 3rd Edition.*

Andrews, M., Squire, C., & Tamboukou, M. (Eds.). (2013). *Doing narrative research.* Sage.

Ansari, A., Yang, A. (Writers). Matsoukas, M. (Director). (2017, May 12). Thanksgiving (Season 2, Episode 8) [TV series episode]. In A. Ansari. , A. Yang. , M. Schur. , D. Becky. , D. Miner. , L. Waithe. , N. Ackie (Executive Producers), *Master of None.* Alan Yang Pictures. , Oh Brudder Productions. , Fremulon. , 3 Arts Entertainment. , Universal Television.

Assari, S., & Lankarani, M. M. (2016). Race and urbanity alter the protective effect of education but not income on mortality. *Front in Public Health, 4,* 100. https: //doi.org/10.3389/fpubh.2016.00100

Assari, S. (2018). Life expectancy gain due to employment status depends on race, gender, education, and their intersections. *Journal of racial and ethnic health disparities, 5*(2), 375–86.

Assari, S. (2018). Health disparities due to diminished return among black americans: Public policy solutions. *Social Issues and Policy Review, 12*(1), 112–45. http: //dx.doi.org/10.1111/sipr.12042

Ayoubkhani, D., Nafilyan, V., White, C., Goldblatt, P., Gaughan, C., Blackwell, L., Rogers, N., Banerjee, A., Khunti, K., Glickman, M., Humberstone, B., & Diamond, I. (2020). Ethnic minority groups in england and wales—factors affecting the size and timing of elevated COVID- 19 mortality: a retrospective cohort study linking Census and death records. *medRxiv*, 2020.2008.2003.20167122. https: //doi.org/10.1101/2020.08.03.20167122

Baldwin, J. (2017, February 3). *I Am Not Your Negro clip—Future of America*. YouTube. https: //www.youtube.com/watch?v=nAmL3F5uylo

Balsamo, M. (2020, December 1). *Disputing trump, barr says no widespread election fraud*. AP NEWS. https: //apnews.com/article/barr-no-widespread-election-fraud-b1f1488796c9a98c4b1a9061a6c7f49d

Barrett, L. (1995). African-American slave narratives: Literacy, the body, authority. *American Literary History, 7*(3), 415–42.

Bennett, G. G., Merritt, M. M., Edwards, C. L., & Sollers, John J., I., II. (2004). Perceived racism and affective responses to ambiguous interpersonal interactions among african-american men. *American Behavioral Scientist, 47*(7), 963–76. http: //dx.doi.org/10.1177/0002764203261070

Blessett, B. (2015). Disenfranchisement: Historical underpinnings and contemporary manifestations. *Public Administration Quarterly*, 3–50.

Block, J. & Kremen, A. M. (1996). IQ and ego-resiliency: Conceptual and empirical connections and separateness. *Journal of Personality and Social Psychology*, 70(2), 349–61.

Bloomberg, L. D., & Volpe, M. (2016). *Completing your qualitative dissertation: A road map from beginning to end.* Sage Publications.

Bonanno, G. A., Wortman, C. B., Lehman, D. R., Tweed, R. G., Haring, M., Sonnega, J., Carr, D., . . . (2002). Resilience to loss and chronic grief: A prospective study from preloss to 18-months postloss. *Journal of Personality and Social Psychology, 83*(5), 1150–164.

Bonanno GA, Brewin CR, Kaniasty K, LaGreca AM. (2010). Weighing the costs of disaster: consequences, risks, and resilience in individuals, families, and communities. *Psychological Science in the Public Interest.* In press

Bonanno, G. A., Westphal, M., & Mancini, A. D. (2011). Resilience to loss and potential trauma. *Annual Review of Clinical Psychology, 7,* 511–35. doi: http: //dx.doi.org/10.1146/annurev-clinpsy-032210–104526

Bonanno, G. A., Romero, S. A., & Klein, S. I. (2015). The temporal elements of psychological resilience: An integrative framework for the study of individuals, families, and communities. *Psychological Inquiry, 26,* 139–69. https: //doi.org/10.1080/1047840X.2015.992677

Booker, B. B. (2018, August). *In baltimore, the gap Between white and black homeownership persists.* NPR. https: //www.npr.org/2018/08/07/632497683/in-baltimore-the-gap-between-white-and-black-homeownership-persists

Bowleg, L. (2020). "We're not all in this together: On COVID-19, Intersectionality, and structural inequality." *American Journal of Public Health*110, no. 7 (July 1, 2020): pp. 917-917.

Brandon, D. T., Isaac, L. A., & LaVeist, T. A. (2013). The legacy of tuskegee and trust in medical care: Is Tuskegee responsible for race differences in mistrust of medical care? In T. A. LaVeist, & L. A. Isaac (Eds.), *2nd ed. ; race, ethnicity, and health: A public health reader* (*2nd ed.*) (2nd ed. ed. , pp. 557–68, Chapter xxv, 819 Pages) Jossey-Bass/Wiley, Hoboken, NJ. Retrieved from https: //www2.1ib.ku.edu/login? url=https:

//www.proquest.com/books/legacy-tuskegee-trust-medical-care-is-responsible/docview/1805491883/se-2? accountid=14556

Braun, V. and Clarke, V. (2013) *Successful qualitative research: A practical guide for beginners*. Sage Publication.

Braun, V., & Clarke, V. (2014). What can "thematic analysis" offer health and wellbeing researchers? *International Journal of Qualitative Student Health Well-being.*

Brender, J. D., Maantay, J. A., & Chakraborty, J. (2011). Residential proximity to environmental hazards and adverse health outcomes. *American journal of public health, 101*(S1), S37-S52.Brinkmann, S. (2014). Unstructured and semi-structured interviewing. *The Oxford Handbook of Qualitative Research*, 277–99.

Brockell, G. (2019, September 15). *William f. buckley jr. vs. james baldwin: A racial showdown on the american dream*. Washington Post. https: //www.washingtonpost.com/history/2019/09/15/william-f-buckley-jr-vs-james-baldwin-racial-showdown-american-dream/

Brooks, S. K., Webster, R. K., Smith, L. E., Woodland, L., Wessely, S., Greenberg, N., & Rubin, G. J. (2020). The psychological impact of quarantine and how to reduce it: Rapid review of the evidence. *The lancet, 395*(10227), 912–20.

Brown, R. C. (1937). The National Negro Health Week Movement. *The Journal of Negro Education, 6*(3), 553–64. https: //doi.org/10.2307/2292305

Burton, M. S., Cooper, A. A., Feeny, N. C., & Zoellner, L. A. (2015). The enhancement of natural resilience in trauma interventions. *Journal of Contemporary Psychotherapy, 45,* 193–204. http: //dx.doi.org/10.1007/ s10879–015–9302–7

Castelnuovo, G., De Giorgio, A., Manzoni, G. M., Treadway, D. C., & Mohiyeddini, C. (2020). Psychological, behavioral, and interpersonal effects and clinical implications for health systems of the coronavirus (COVID-19) pandemic: A call for research.

Frontiers in Psychology, 11, 3. doi: http: //dx.doi.org/10.3389/fpsyg.2020.02146

Center for Disease Control and Prevention. (2018). Lead: Information for workers, health problems caused by lead. CDC. https: //www.cdc.gov/niosh/topics/lead/health.html

Chaney, C. (2009). Boys to men: How perceptions of manhood influence the romantic partnership of black men. *The Western Journal of Black Studies, 33*, 110–22

Chavez, N. (2020). *The year america confronted racism.* CNN. https: //edition.cnn.com/interactive/2020/12/us/america-racism-2020/

Chavez, N. C. (2021, January 11). *BLM vs capitol protests: This was the police response when it was black protesters on DC streets last year.* CNN. https: //edition.cnn.com/2021/01/07/us/police-response-black-lives-matter-protest-us-capitol/index.html

Che, M., Rodriguez, O. (2021) Dudley gets shot (Season 1, Episode 3). Michaels, L, That damn michael che.

Chia-Chen Chen, A., Keith, V. M., Airriess, C., Li, W., & Leong, K. J. (2007). Economic vulnerability, discrimination, and hurricane katrina: Health among black katrina survivors in eastern new orleans. *Journal of the American Psychiatric Nurses Association, 13*(5), 257–66. doi: http: //dx.doi.org/10.1177/1078390307307260

Cicchetti, D. (1984). The emergence of developmental psychopathology. *Child development, 55*(1), 1–7.

Clark, K.B., Clark M.P, (1950). Emotional factors in racial identification and preference in negro children. *Journal of Negro Education.*

Clegg, S. R., & Bailey, J. R. (Eds.) (2008). . (Vols. 1-4). SAGE Publications, Inc., https://dx.doi.org/10.4135/9781412956246

Cole, L. J., (2020). *Snow on tha bluff.* https: //www.azlyrics.com/lyrics/jcole/snowonthabluff.html

Cooke, P. J., Melchert, T. P., & Connor, K. (2016). Measuring well-being: A review of instruments. *The Counseling Psychologist, 44*(5), 730–57.

Cooper, S. M., Thomas, A., & Bamishigbin, O. (2021). Black american fathers employed in higher-risk contexts for contracting COVID-19: Implications for individual wellbeing and work-family spillover. *American Journal of Men's Health, 15*(2), 15579883211005617.

Corbie-Smith, G., Wolfe, M. K., Hoover, S. M., & Dave, G. (2021). Centering equity and community in the recovery of the COVID-19 pandemic. *North Carolina medical journal, 82*(1), 62–67.

Cummings, W. J., Garrison, G. A., & Sergent, J. S. (2021, January 6). *By the numbers: President donald trump's failed efforts to overturn the election*. USA Today News. https: //eu.usatoday.com/in-depth/news/politics/elections/2021/01/06/trumps-failed-efforts-overturn-election-numbers/4130307001/

Curry T. J. (2017). *The man-not: race class genre and the dilemmas of black manhood.* Temple University Press.

Crimmins, E. M., Shim, H., Zhang, Y. S., & Kim, J. K. (2019). Differences between men and women in mortality and the health dimensions of the morbidity process. *Clinical Chemistry, 65*(1), 135–45. https: //doi.org/10.1373/clinchem.2018.288332

Cross, W. E. (1971). Negro-to-black conversion experience. *Black World,20,* 13–29.

Cross, W. E., Jr. (1991). *Shades of black: Diversity in african-american identity*. Temple University Press.

Cross, W. E. (1994). Nigrescence theory: Historical and explanatory notes. *Journal of Vocational Behaviour, 44*, 119–19.

Day, A. (2015). *Rise up. https: //genius.com/Andra-day-rise-up-lyrics*

Debate: Baldwin vs. buckley. Film and Media Archive, Washington University in St. Louis, Library of Congress, American Archive of Public Broadcasting (GBH and the Library of Congress), Boston,

MA and Washington, DC. Retrieved from http: //americanarchive.org/catalog/cpb-aacip-151-sn00z71m54

Delgado, R., & Stefancic, J. (2017). Chapter II. Hallmark critical race theory themes. In *Critical Race Theory (Third Edition)* (pp. 19-43). New York University Press.

Dell'Osso, L., Carmassi, C., Conversano, C., Capanna, C., Stratta, P., & Rossi, A. (2011). Full and partial PTSD among 475 young adult survivors 20 months after the l'aquila 2009 earthquake: impact of loss events. ECNP 2011. In *ECNP 2011.*

Dews, F. (2021, February 26). Charts of the week: Black men's life expectancy; student debt and black households; struggling families. *Brookings*. https: //www.brookings.edu/blog/brookings-now/2021/02/26/charts-of-the-week-black-mens-life-expectancy-student-debt-and-black-households-struggling-families/

Department of Homeland Security. (2020). *Homeland threat assessment, 2020.* dhs.gov. Retrieved September 15, 2022, from https: //www.dhs.gov/sites/default/files/publications/2020_10_06_homeland-threat-assessment.pdf

Di Giuseppe, M., Gemignani, A., Conversano, C. (2020). Psychological resources against the traumatic experience of COVID-19. *Clinical Neuropsychiatry,* 17 (2), 85–87.

Disparities in wealth by race and ethnicity in the 2019 survey of consumer finances. (n.d.). Retrieved April 24, 2021, from https: //www.federalreserve.gov/econres/notes/feds-notes/disparities-in-wealth-by-race-and-ethnicity-in-the-2019-survey-of-consumer-finances-20200928. htm

Dreier, P. (2013, April 11). *The real story of baseballs integration that you won't see in 42.* The Atlantic. https: //www.theatlantic.com/entertainment/archive/2013/04/the-real-story-of-baseballs-integration-that-you-wont-see-in-i-42-i/274886/

Du Bois, W. E. B. (1968). The souls of black folk; essays and sketches. Chicago, A. G. McClurg, 1903. New York: *Johnson Reprint Corp.*

Dunbar, A & Nicole E. Jones, N.E. (2021). Race, police, and the pandemic: considering the role of race in public health policing. *Ethnic and Racial Studies, 44* (5), 773–82. https:// doi: 10.1080/01419870.2020.1851381

Duncan, D.T., Kawachi, I. (Eds). (2018). *Neighborhoods and health.* (2nd ed). Oxford University Press, New York, NY.

Easwran, E. (2007). *The bhagavad gita* (Trans; 2nd ed.). The Blue Mountain Center of Mediation.

Eberhardt, J. L., Goff, P. A., Purdie, V. J., & Davies, P. G. (2004). Seeing black: race, crime, and visual processing. *Journal of Personality and Social Psychology, 87*(6), 876.

Edwards, F. L., & Thomson, G. (2010). The legal creation of raced space: The subtle and ongoing discrimination created through jim crow laws. *Berkeley Journal of African-American Law and Policy, 12,* 145–68.

Evans, M., and K. Bauer. 2020, May 26th. Chicago police only arrested people for social distancing violations on the south and west sides, data shows. *Block Club Chicago.* Accessed August 28, 2020. https: //blockclubchicago.org/2020/05/26/ chicago-police-only-arrested-people-for-social-distancing-on-the-south-and-west- sides-data-shows/.

Falicov, C. J. (2014). Psychotherapy and supervision as cultural encounters: The multidimensional ecological comparative approach framework.

Fishman, L. T. (2006). The black bogeyman and white self-righteousness. In: Mann, C.R, Zatz, M. S and Rodriguez, N. (eds) *Images of color, images of crime.* New York: Oxford University Press, 197–211.

Feder, A., Fred-Torres, S., Southwick, S. M., & Charney, D. S. (2019). The biology of human resilience: Opportunities for enhancing resilience across the lifespan. *Biological Psychiatry, 86,* 443–53. http: //dx.doi.org/10.1016/j.biopsych.2019.07.012

Ferdinand, K. C., Nedunchezhian, S., & Reddy, T. K. (2020). The COVID-19 and influenza "twindemic": Barriers to influenza vaccination and potential acceptance of SARS-CoV2 vaccination in african americans. *Journal of the National Medical Association, 112*(6), 681–87.

Fergus, S., & Zimmerman, M. A. (2005). Adolescent resilience: A framework for understanding healthy development in the face of risk. *Annual Review of Public Health, 26*, 399–419. doi: http: //dx.doi.org/10.1146/annurev.publhealth.26.021304.144357

Foste, Z. (2020). The enlightenment narrative: White student leaders' preoccupation with racial innocence. *Journal of Diversity in Higher Education, 13*(1), 33.

Frank, A. (2010). *Letting stories breathe: A socio-narratology.* Chicago: University of Chicago Press.

Fraser, M. (1997). *Risk and resilience in childhood.* Washington, DC: NASW Press.

Fraser, M. W., & Galinsky, M. J. (1997). Toward a resilience-based model of practice. In M. W. Fraser (Ed.), *Risk and resilience in childhood* (pp. 265–76). Washington, DC: NASW Press.

Fraser, M. W., Richman, J. M., & Galinsky, M. J. (1999). Risk, protection, and resilience: Toward a conceptual framework for social work practice. *Social Work Research, 23*(3), 129–208.

Galily Y. (2021). The coronavirus pandemic as a game-changer: When NBA players forced america to think. Again. *Frontiers in Psychology, 11*, 600267. https: //doi.org/10.3389/fpsyg.2020.600267

Gates H. L. & Yacovone D. (2013). *The african americans: many rivers to cross.* SmileyBooks. Retrieved November 23 2022 from https: //www.overdrive.com/search? q=B79648F8–36FF-497A-8D22–1916917302D5.

Georges, J. M. (2005). Linking nursing theory and practice: A critical feminist approach. *Advances in Nursing Science*, 28, 50–57.

Gramlich, J. (2020, May 6). Black imprisonment rate in the U. S. has fallen by a third since 2006. *Pew Research Center.* https: //www.pewresearch.org/fact-tank/2020/05/06/share-of-black-white-hispanic-americans-in-prison-2018-vs-2006/

Greene, R. R. (2002). Resilience: Theory and research for social work practice. Washington, DC: *NASW Press.*

Greene, R. R., Galambos, C., & Lee, Y. (2003). Resilience theory: Theoretical and professional conceptualizations. *Journal of Human Behavior in the Social Environment, 8*(4), 75–91. doi: http: //dx.doi.org/10.1300/J137v08n04_05

Greene, R.R., Colleen Galambos D.W., & Lee D. W. (2004) Resilience theory. *Journal of Human Behavior in the Social Environment,* 8:4, 75–91, doi: 10.1300/J137v08n04_05

Gross, T. (2017). *A "forgotten history" of how the u.s. government segregated america.* NPR. https: //www.npr.org/2017/05/03/526655831/a-forgotten-history-of-how-the-u-s-government-segregated-america

Gubrium, J. F., & Holstein, J. A. (1997). *The new language of qualitative method.* New York, NY: Oxford University Press.

Gusau, S. B., Lachal, J., Radjack, R., Carretier, E., Minassian, S., Benoit, L., & Moro, M. R. (2020). Adolescent psychiatric disorders during the COVID-19 pandemic and lockdown. *Psychiatry Research, 113264.* https: //doi.org/10.1016/j. psychres.2020.113264

Guy, T. C. (2014). The (end)angered black male swimming against the current. *New Directions for Adult and Continuing Education, 2014*(144), 15–26.

Gwadz, M., Campos, S., Freeman, R., Cleland, C. M., Wilton, L., Sherpa, D., Leonard, N. R. (2021). Black and latino persons living with hiv evidence risk and resilience in the context of covid-19: A mixed-methods study of the early phase of the pandemic. *AIDS and Behavior,* doi: http: //dx.doi.org/10.1007/s10461–021–03177–0

Hackman, H. W., & Rauscher, L. (2004). A pathway to access for all: Exploring the connections between universal instructional design and social justice education. *Equity & Excellence in Education* (37), 114–23.

Hall, E. H., & King, G. C. (1982). Working with the strengths of black families. *Child Welfare:*

Hall, M. F. (1997). The "war on drugs": A continuation of the war on the african-american family. *Smith College Studies in Social Work, 67*(3), 609–21. doi: http: //dx.doi.org/10.1080/00377319709517509

Haller, John S. (1971). *Outcasts from evolution; scientific attitudes of racial inferiority, 1859-1900.* Urbana : University of Illinois Press.

Hamilton, B. E., Martin, J. A., & Ventura, S. J. (2010). Births: Preliminary data for 2008. *National Vital Statistics Reports, 59*(3), 1–19.

Hammond, W.P., & Mattis. J. S. (2005). Being a man about it: Manhood meaning among african american men. *Psychology of Men & Masculinities, 6,* 114–26.

Hardy, K. V. (2013). Healing the hidden wounds of racial trauma. *Reclaiming Children and Youth, 22*(1), 24.

Hardy, K. V. (2016, June). *The view from black america. Networker Symposium.* retrieved from YouTube: https: //www.youtube.com/watch? v=i26A50ecUWM&t=8s

Hardy, K. V., & Laszloffy, T. A. (2000). The development of children and families of color: A supplemental framework. In W. C. Nichols, M. A. Pace-Nichols, D. S. Becvar & A. Y. Napier (Eds.), *Handbook of family development and intervention; handbook of family development and intervention* (pp. 109–28, Chapter xxii, 482 Pages) John Wiley & Sons, Inc. , Hoboken, NJ. Retrieved from https: //www2.1ib.ku.edu/login? url=https: //www.proquest.com/books/development-children-families-color-supplemental/docview/619501055/se-2? accountid=14556

Harold, C., & DeLuca, K. M. (2005). Behold the corpse: Violent images and the case of emmett till. *Rhetoric & Public Affairs 8*(2), 263–86. doi:10.1353/rap.2005.0075.

Harper, S., Lynch, J., Burris, S., & Smith, G. D. (2007). Trends in the black– white life expectancy gap in the united states, 1983–2003. *Journal of the American Medical Society*, 297, 1224–1232.

Helms, J. E. (1997). Toward a model of white racial identity development. *College Student Development and Academic Life: Psychological, Intellectual, Social and Moral Issues*, 49–66.

Hermann, P., & Thompson, S. (2021, April 8). *D. C. medical examiner releases cause of death for four people who died during Capitol riot.* Washington Post. https: //www.washingtonpost.com/local/public-safety/trump-riot-death-medical-exainer/2021/04/07/53806608–97cf-11eb-a6d0–13d207aadb78_story.html

Hernandez-Wolfe, P., Killian, K., Engstrom, D., & Gangsei, D. (2015). Vicarious resilience, vicarious trauma, and awareness of equity in trauma work. *Journal of Humanistic Psychology, 55*(2), 153–72. doi: http: //dx.doi.org/10.1177/0022167814534322

Hobfoll SE. 2002. Social and psychological resources and adaptation. *Review of General. Psychology.* 6:307–24

Hogan, V. K., and C. D. Ferre. 2001. "The social context of pregnancy for african american women: Implications for the study and prevention of adverse perinatal outcomes." *Maternal and Child Health Journal*, 5 (2): 67–69. doi:10.1023/A:1011360813893.

Hooks, B. (2004). *We real cool: Black men and masculinity*. Psychology Press.

Hopper, E. K. (2017). Polyvictimization and developmental trauma adaptations in sex trafficked youth. Journal of Child and Adolescent Trauma, 10(2), 161–73. https: //doi.org/10.1007/s40653–016–0114-z

Howard, T. (2008). Who really cares? The disenfranchisement of african american males in preK-12 schools: A critical race theory perspective. *Teachers College Record, 110*(5), 954–85.

Hughes, L. (1957). *Still here.* https: //www.best-poems.net/langston_hughes/still_here.html

Hunter, A.G., & Davis, J. E. (1992). An exploration of afro-american men's conceptualization of manhood. *Gender & Society, 6,* 464–79.

Isaksen, S. G., Dorval, K. B., & Treffinger, D. J. (2011). Creative approaches to problem solving: A framework for innovation and change. Sage Publications.

Jackson, C. (2021, August 17). What Is Redlining? *The New York Times*. https://www.nytimes.com/2021/08/17/realestate/what-is-redlining.html

Jackson, J. L. (1990). Suicide trends of blacks and whites by sex and age. In D. S. Ruiz (Ed.), *Handbook of Mental Health Disorder Among Black Americans* (pp. 95–109). New York: Green- wood Press.

Johns hopkins aramco healthcare. (2020). *COVID-19 mental health tool kit*. Retrieved from https: //www.jhah.com/en/new-coronavirus/mental- health-tool-kit

Johns hopkins university and medicine coronavirus resource center (n. d.). Maps and trends: Racial data transparency: State COVID-19 data by race. Retrieved from https: //coronavirus.jhu.edu/data/racial-data-transparency

Johnson-Ahorlu, R. (2017). Efficient social justice: How critical race theory research can inform social movement strategy development. *The Urban Review, 49*(5), 729–45. doi: http: //dx.doi.org/10.1007/s11256–017–0419–8

Johnson, E. H. (1990). The deadly emotions. New York: Praeger. *Journal of Policy, Practice, and Program, 61*(8), 536–44. Retrieved from https: //www2.1ib.ku.edu/login? url=https: //www.proquest.com/scholarly-journals/working-with-strengths-black-families/docview/616777950/se-2? accountid=14556

Jones, N. (1994). *NY state of mind. https: //genius.com/Nas-ny-state-of-mind-lyrics*

Jordan, A. H., Lovett, B. J., & Sweeton, J. L. (2012). The social psychology of black–white interracial interactions: Implications for culturally competent clinical practice. *Journal of Multicultural Counseling and Development, 40*(3), 132–43.

Kalina, P. (2020). Performative allyship. *Technium Social Sciences Journal, 11*, 478-[xliv].

Kane, M. L. (2021). *What one black man wants kansans to know about watching the insurrection.* Kansas Reflector. https: //kansasreflector.com/2021/01/23/what-one-black-man-wants-kansans-to-know-about-watching-the-insurrection/

Kaplan, J., & B. Hardy. (2020). Early data shows black people are being disproportionally arrested for social distancing violations. *ProPublica.* Accessed May 28th, 2020. https: //www.propublica.org/article/in-some-of-ohios-most- populous areas-black-people-were-at-least-4-times-as-likely-to-be-charged-with- stay-at-homeviolations-as-whites.

Kaur, H. C. (2020, September 5). *About 93% of racial justice protests in the US have been peaceful, a new report finds.* CNN. https: //edition.cnn.com/2020/09/04/us/blm-protests-peaceful-report-trnd/index.html?fbclid=IwAR1BFIeGt_HvJKfeeXzGpAwPKevQueJchfgSkklI__EZVNmLepxAqchqTFQ

Kendi, I. X. (2022, June 10). *Ibram X. Kendi: My Family's Doll Test.* The Atlantic. Retrieved October 15, 2022, from https: //www.theatlantic.com/magazine/archive/2022/07/doll-test-history-racial-segregation-toy-diversity/638442/

Keyes, C. L. (2009). The black–white paradox in health: Flourishing in the face of social inequality and discrimination. *Journal of Personality, 77*(6), 1677–1706.

Keyes, C. L., & Haidt, J. (2003). *Flourishing.* American Psychological Association.

Keyes, C. L., Wissing, M., Potgieter, J. P., Temane, M., Kruger, A., & van Rooy, S. (2008). Evaluation of the mental health continuum-short form (MHC-SF) in setswana-speaking south africans. *Clinical Psychology & Psychotherapy,* 15, 181–92.

Khanna, N. (2010). "If you're half black, you're just black": Reflected appraisals and the persistence of the one-drop rule. *The Sociological Quarterly*, 51, 96–121, DOI: 10.1111/j.1533–8525.2009.01162. x

Kira, I. A., Shuwiekh, H. A., Ahmed, S. A. E., Ebada, E. E., Tantawy, S. F., Waheep, N. N., & Ashby, J. S. (2022). Coping with COVID-19 prolonged and cumulative stressors: The case example of egypt. *International Journal of Mental Health and Addiction*, 1–22.

Kishi, R., Stall, H., Wolfson, A., & Jones, S. (2022, September 5). *A year of racial justice protests: Key trends in demonstrations supporting the BLM movement*. ACLED. https://acleddata.com/2021/05/25/a-year-of-racial-justice-protests-key-trends-in-demonstrations-supporting-the-blm-movement/

Koch, J. W. (2019). Racial minorities' trust in government and government decisionmakers. *Social Science Quarterly, 100*(1), 19–37. doi: http: //dx.doi.org/10.1111/ssqu.12548

Krieger, N. (2020). ENOUGH: COVID-19, structural racism, police brutality, plutocracy, climate change-and time for health justice, democratic governance, and an equitable, sustainable future. *American Journal of Public Health, 110*(11), 1620–1623. doi: http: //dx.doi.org/10.2105/AJPH.2020.305886

Krieger, N. (2011). *Epidemiology and the People's Health*. Oxford University Press, New York, NY.

Lamar, K. (2015). King Kunta [Song]. *On To pimp a butterfly*. Top Dawg; Aftermath; Interscope.

Lartey, J. By the numbers: US police kill more in days than other countries do in years. *The Guardian*, (9 June 2015). http: //www.theguardian.com/us-news/2015/jun/09/the- counted-police-killings-us-vs-other-countries.

Leary, Joy DeGruy. (2017). *Post traumatic slave syndrome: America's legacy of enduring injury and healing*. Milwaukie, Oregon: Uptone Press.

Lewis D. L. (19941993). *W.e.b. dubois: biography of a race 1868–1919* (1st Owl book). H. Holt.

Levinson, J. D., & Young, D. (2009). "Different shades of bias: Skin tone, implicit racial bias, and judgments of ambiguous evidence." *West Virginia Law Review*. 112, 307– 338.

Lincoln, Y. S., & Guba, E. G. (1986). But is it rigorous? Trustworthiness and authenticity in naturalistic evaluation. *New Directions for Program Evaluation*, 73–83.

Liu, X., Kakade, M., Fuller, C. J., Fan, B., Fang, Y., Kong, J., Guan, Z., & Wu, P. (2012). Depression after exposure to stressful events: lessons learned from the severe acute respiratory syndrome epidemic. *Comprehensive Psychiatry, 53*(1), 15–23.

Lopez, S. J., Prosser, E. C., Edwards, L. M., Magyar-Moe, J. L., Neufeld, J. E., & Rasmussen, H. N. (2002). Putting positive psychology in a multicultural context. *Handbook of positive psychology*, 700–714.

Magyar-Moe, J. L. (2014). Infusing multiculturalism and positive psychology in psychotherapy. In *Perspectives on the Intersection of Multiculturalism and Positive Psychology* (pp. 235–49). Springer, Dordrecht.

Mahalik, J. R., Pierre, M. R., & Wan, S. S. C. (2006). Examining racial identity and masculinity as correlates of self-esteem and psychological distress in black men. *Journal of Multicultural Counseling and Development, 34*(2), 94–104. doi: http: //dx.doi.org.www2.1ib.ku.edu/10.1002/j.2161–912.2006. tb00030. x

Major, B. C., Le Nguyen, K. D., Lundberg, K. B., & Fredrickson, B. L. (2018). Well-being correlates of perceived positivity resonance: Evidence from trait and episode-level assessments. *Personality and Social Psychology Bulletin, 44*(12), 1631–1647.

Manchia, M., Gathier, A. W., Yapici-Eser, H., Schmidt, M. V., de Quervain, D., van Amelsvoort, T., . . . & Vinkers, C. H. (2022). The impact of the prolonged COVID-19 pandemic on stress resilience and mental health: A critical review across waves. *European Neuropsychopharmacology, 55*, 22–83.

Mansfield, A. K., Addis, M. E., & Mahalik, J. R. (2003). "Why won't he go to the doctor?": The psychology of men's help seeking. *International Journal of Mens Health, 2,* 93–110.

Martino, G., Catalano, A., Bellone, F., Russo, G.T., Vicario, C.m. , Lasco, A., Quattropani, M.C., Morabito, N. (2019a). As time goes by: Anxiety negatively affects the perceived quality of life in patients with type 2 diabetes of long duration. *Frontiers in Psychology,* 10:1–8. Doi: 10.3389/fpsyg.2019.01779.

Massey, D.S., & Denton, N. (1993). *American apartheid: Segregation and the making of the underclass.* Cambridge, MA: Harvard University Press.

Masten, A. (1994). Resilience in individual development: Successful adaptation despite risk and adversity. In Wang M. C. & Gordon E. W. (Eds.), *Educational resilience in inner-city America: Challenges and prospects* (pp. 3–25). Hillsdale, NJ: Lawrence Erlbaum Associates.

Masten, A. S. (1989). Resilience in development: Implications of the study of successful adaptation for developmental psychopathology. In Cicchetti, D. (Ed.), *The emergence of a discipline: Vol. 1. Rochester Symposium on Developmental Psychopathology* (pp. 261–94). Hillsdale, NJ: Erlbaum.

Masten, A. S. (2018). Resilience theory and research on children and families: Past, present, and promise. *Journal of Family Theory & Review, 10,* 12–31. http: //dx.doi.org/10.1111/jftr.12255

Mathews, T. J., & MacDorman, M. F. (2008). "Infant mortality statistics from the 2005 period linked birth/infant death data set." *National Vital Statistics Reports* 57 (2): 1–32.

McClure, E., Feinstein, L., Cordoba, E., Douglas, C., Emch, M., Robinson, W., Galea, S., Aiello, A. E. (2019). The legacy of redlining in the effect of foreclosures on detroit residents' self-rated health. *Health & Place, 55,* 9–19. doi: http: //dx.doi.org/10.1016/j.healthplace.2018.10.004

McCubbin, H. I., McCubbin, M. A., Thompson, A. I., & Thompson, E. A. (1998). Resiliency in ethnic families: A conceptual model for predicting family adjustment and adaptation. In H. I. McCubbin, E. A. Thompson, A. I. Thompson, & J. E. Fromer (Eds.), *Resiliency in Native American and Immigrant Families* (pp. 3–48). Thousand Oaks, CA: Sage.

McKinney, T. M. (2021, March 10). Racial trauma in film: How viewers can address re-traumatization. https: //counseling.northwestern.edu/blog/racial-trauma-retraumatization-film/

McLeod, J. (2011). *Qualitative research in counselling and psychotherapy.* Los Angeles: SAGE.

Menakem, R. (2017). *My grandmother's hands.* Central Recovery Press.

Merriam-Webster. (2011). racism. in *Merriam-Webster.com.* From https: //www.merriam-webster.com (10 May 2021).

Milner, C. M. (2020, July 6). *Black americans on mental health, trauma, and resilience.* STAT. https: //www.statnews.com/2020/07/06/it-just-weighs-on-your-psyche-black-americans-on-mental-health-trauma-and-resilience/

Mincey, K.D., Alfonso, M., Hackney, A., & Luque, J. (2014). Understanding masculinity in undergraduate african american men: A qualitative study. *American Journal of Men's Health,* 8, 387–98.

Mishler, E. G. (1986). The analysis of interview-narratives. In T. R. Sarbin (Ed.), *Narrative psychology: The storied nature of human conduct* (pp. 233–55). Praeger Publishers/Greenwood Publishing Group.

National Academies of Sciences, Engineering, and Medicine. 2020. *Framework for equitable allocation of COVID-19 vaccine.* Washington, DC: The National Academies Press. https: //doi.org/10.17226/25917

National negro health week: Health is a human right [Race and Place in America]. *Georgia State University Library Exhibits*. (n.d.). https: //exhibits.library.gsu.edu/current/exhibits/show/health-is-a-human-right/healthcare-for-all/national-negro-health-week

Ndugga, N., Pham, O., Hill, L., Artiga, S., Alam, R., & Parker, N. (2021, May 26). *Latest data on COVID-19 vaccinations race/ethnicity*. KFF. https: //www.kff.org/coronavirus-covid-19/issue-brief/latest-data-on-covid-19-vaccinations-race-ethnicity/

NPR. (2017, May). *'The color of law' details how U. S. housing policies created segregation.* All things considered. https: //www.npr.org/2017/05/17/528822128/the-color-of-law-details-how-u-s-housing-policies-created-segregation.

NPR. (2018, April 11). *Housing segregation and redlining in america: A short history.* Code Switch. *NPR* [Video]. YouTube. https: //www.youtube.com/watch? v=05FBJyqfoLM

Nuttman-Shwartz, O., & Green, O. (2021). Resilience truths: Trauma resilience workers' points of view toward resilience in continuous traumatic situations. *International Journal of Stress Management, 28*(1), 1–10. doi: http: //dx.doi.org/10.1037/str0000223

Oliver, A., Andemeskel, G., King, C. R., Wallace, L., McDougal, S., Monteiro, K. P., & Ben-Zeev, A. (2017). 'I'm black and I'm proud': A majority ecological context protects affective aspects of black identity under stereotype threat. *Race and Social Problems, 9*(4), 313–20. doi: http: //dx.doi.org/10.1007/s12552–017–9216-y

Oshio, A., Taku, K., Hirano, M., & Saeed, G. (2018). Resilience and big five personality traits: A meta-analysis. *Personality and Individual Differences,* 127, 54–60. https: //doi.org/10.1016/j.paid.2018.01.048

Ortega-Williams, A., Beltràn, R., Schultz, K., Ru-Glo Henderson, z. , Colón, L., & Teyra, C. (2021). An integrated historical trauma and posttraumatic growth framework: A cross-cultural exploration. *Journal of Trauma & Dissociation, 22, 220–40.*

Owusu-Bempah, A. (2017). Race and policing in historical context: Dehumanization and the policing of black people in the 21st century. *Theoretical Criminology*, 21(1), 23–34.

Parham, T. A., & Helms, J. E. (1985). Relation of racial identity attitudes to self-actualization and affective states of Black students. *Journal of Counseling Psychology, 32*(3), 431.

Patton, T. O. (2001). "Ally McBeal" and her homies: The reification of white stereotypes of the other. *Journal of Black Studies*, 229–60.

PeConga, E. K., Gauthier, G. M., Holloway, A., Walker, R. S. W., Rosencrans, P. L., Zoellner, L. A., & Bedard-Gilligan, M. (2020). Resilience is spreading: Mental health within the COVID-19 pandemic. *Psychological Trauma: Theory, Research, Practice, and Policy, 12*, S47-S48. doi: http: //dx.doi.org/10.1037/tra0000874

Penner, L. A., Blair, I. V., Albrecht, T. L., Dovidio, J. F., Fiske, S. T., Borgida, E., & Major, B. (2014). Reducing racial health care disparities: A social psychological analysis. *Policy Insights from the Behavioral and Brain Sciences, 1*(1), 204–12. https: //doi.org/10.1177/2372732214548430

Pierre, M. R., & Mahalik, J. R. (2005). Examining african self-consciousness and black racial identity as predictors of black men's psychological well-being. *Cultural Diversity and Ethnic Minority Psychology, 11*(1), 28–40. doi: http: //dx.doi.org/10.1037/1099–9809.11.1.28

Pincus, F. L. (2019). From individual to structural discrimination. In *Race and Ethnic Conflict* (pp. 120–24). Routledge.

Pitcan, M., Park-Taylor, J., & Hayslett, J. (2018). Black men and racial microaggressions at work. *The Career Development Quarterly, 66*(4), 300. doi: http: //dx.doi.org/10.1002/cdq.12152

Pollitt, P. A. (1996). From national Negro health week to national public health week. *Journal of Community Health, 21*, 401-408.

Polkinghorne, D.E., (1995) Narrative configuration in qualitative analysis, *International Journal of Qualitative Studies in Education*, 8, 5–23, DOI: *10.1080/0951839950080103*

Prout, T. A., Zilcha-Mano, S., Aafjes-van Doorn, K., Békés, V., Christman-Cohen, I., Whistler, K., Kui, T., & Di Giuseppe, M. (2020). Identifying predictors of psychological distress during COVID-19: A machine learning approach. *Frontiers in Psychology, 11*, 586202. https: //doi.org/10.3389/fpsyg.2020.586202

Rando, T. A. (1997). Vicarious bereavement. In S. Strack (Ed.), Death and the quest for meaning: Essays in honor of Herman Feifel (pp. 257–74). Northdale, NJ: Jason Aronson.

Ray, R. R., & Gibbons, A. G. (2022, March 9). *Why are states banning critical race theory*? Brookings. https: //www.brookings.edu/blog/fixgov/2021/07/02/why-are-states-banning-critical-race-theory/

Reverby SM (2021) Racism, disease, and vaccine refusal: People of color are dying for access to COVID-19 vaccines. *PLoS Biol* 19(3): e3001167. https: //doi.org/10.1371/journal.pbi0.3001167

Rhoden, W. C. (2006). *$40 million slaves: The rise, fall, and redemption of the black athlete.* Three Rivers Press.

Reid, J. A., Haskell, R. A., Dillahunt-Aspillaga, C., Thor, J. A. (2013). Contemporary review of empirical and clinical studies of trauma bonding in violent or exploitative relationships. International Journal of Psychology Research, 8(1), 37–73.

Riehm KE, Brenneke SG, Adams LB, Gilan D, Lieb K, Kunzler AM, Smail EJ, Holingue C, Stuart EA, Kalb LG, Thrul J.(2021). Association between psychological resilience and changes in mental distress during the COVID-19 pandemic. *Journal of Affective Disorders, 282,* 381–85.

Riessman, C. K. (2008). *Narrative methods for the human sciences.* Sage.

Ruiz, N. G., Horowitz, J. M., & Tamir, C. (2020). Many black and asian americans say they have experienced discrimination amid the COVID-19 outbreak. *Pew Research Center, 1.*

Schmidt, H., Weintraub, R., Williams, M. A., Miller, K., Buttenheim, A., Sadecki, E. Wu, S., Doiphode, A., Nagpal, N., Gostin, L. O., & Shen, A. A. (2021). Equitable allocation of COVID-19 vaccines in the united states. *Nature Medicine*, 1–10.

Scott-Heron, G., (1970). Whitey on the moon [Song]. On *Small talk at 125th and Lenox.* https: //genius.com/Gil-scott-heron-whitey-on-the-moon-annotated

Seery, M. D. (2011). Resilience: A silver lining to experiencing adverse life events? Current directions in psychological science, 20(6), 390–94. https: //doi.org/10.1177/0963721411424740

Shakur, T., (1989). *The rose that grew from concrete. https: //genius.com/2pac-the-rose-that-grew-from-concrete-lyrics*

Shapiro, B. S. (2021, January 17). *Eyewitnesses Recount The 1954 Shooting Attack On The U. S. Capitol.* NPR. https: //choice.npr.org/index.html? origin=https: //www.npr.org/2021/01/17/957722906/listen-eyewitnesses-recount-the-1954-shooting-attack-on-the-u-s-capitol

Shapiro, T., (2006). Race, homeownership and wealth. *Washington University Journal of Law & Policy, 20,* [iii]-[iv].

Sherman, A. (2021, May 13). *PolitiFact—The ridiculous claim that those at the capitol Jan. 6 resembled a "normal tourist visit."* Politifact. https: //www.politifact.com/factchecks/2021/may/13/andrew-clyde/ridiculous-claim-those-capitol-jan-6-resembled-nor/

Smith, D. L. (2011). *Less than human: Why we demean, enslave and exterminate others.* New York: Macmillan.

Smith, R. J., J. D. Levinson, and Z. Robinson. (2014). "Implicit white favoritism in the criminal justice system." *Alabama Law Review* 66: 871–925.

Southall, A. (2020, May 29th). *Scrutiny of social-distance policing as 35 of 40 arrested are black.* The New York Times. Accessed June 2, 2020. https: //www.nytimes.com/ 2020/05/07/nyregion/nypd-social-distancing-race-coronavirus.html.

Spohn, C. 2017. "Race and sentencing disparity." Reforming criminal justice: A report of the academy for justice on bridging the gap between scholarship and reform 4, 169–86.

Statista. (2022, September 12). *People shot to death by U. S. police 2017–2022, by race.* Retrieved September 23, 2022, from https: //www.statista.com/statistics/585152/people-shot-to-death-by-us-police-by-race/

Stop W.O.K.E. Act, (U.S.C) 148 HB7 (2022). https://www.flsenate.gov/Session/Bill/2022/148/BillText/Filed/HTML

Strümpfer, D. J. W. (1995). The origins of health and strength: From "salutogenesis" to "fortigenesis." *South African Journal of Psychology, 25,* 81–89.

Sue D. W., Sue D., Neville H. A., & Smith L. (2019). *Counseling the Culturally Diverse.* [VitalSource Bookshelf]. Retrieved from https: //bookshelf.vitalsource.com/#/books/9781119448280/

Sullender, R. S. (2010). Vicarious grieving and the media. *Pastoral Psychology, 59*(2), 191–200. doi: http: //dx.doi.org/10.1007/s11089–009–0227–5

Tedeschi, R. G., & Calhoun, L. G. (2004). Posttraumatic growth: Conceptual foundations and empirical evidence. *Psychological Inquiry, 15*(1), 1–18.

Teti, M., Martin, A. E., Ranade, R., Massie, J., Malebranche, D. J., Tschann, J. M., & Bowleg, L. (2012). "I'ma keep rising. I'ma keep going forward, regardless" exploring black men's resilience amid sociostructural challenges and stressors. *Qualitative Health Research, 22*(4), 524–33.

The Five Stairsteps. (1970). *Ohh Child* [Song]. On Step by step by step. BUDDAH.

The Planetary Society, T. P. (2021, June 18). *How much did the apollo program cost?* The Planetary Society. https: //www.planetary.org/space-policy/cost-of-apollo

The Society for the Psychological Study of Men and Masculinities. (2019). Division 51.

Treadwell, H. M. (2020). The pandemic, racism, and health disparities among african-american men. *American Journal of Men's Health, 14*(4), 3. doi: http: //dx.doi.org/10.1177/1557988320949379

Troy, A. S., Wilhelm, F. H., Shallcross, A. J., & Mauss, I. B. (2010). Seeing the silver lining: Cognitive reappraisal ability moderates the relationship between stress and depressive symptoms. *Emotion, 10*(6), 783–95. https: //doi.org/10.1037/a0020262

U. S. Census Bureau. (2021, April 14). *Poverty rates for blacks and hispanics reached historic lows in 2019.* The United States Census Bureau. https: //www.census.gov/library/stories/2020/09/poverty-rates-for-blacks-and-hispanics-reached-historic-lows-in-2019. html

Ungar, M., & Liebenberg, L. (2011). Assessing resilience across cultures using mixed methods: Construction of the child and youth resilience measure. *Journal of Mixed Methods Research*, 5, 126–49. https: //doi.org/ 10.1177/1558689811400607

Vahratian, A. (2017). *QuickStats: Percentage of adults aged ≥18 years who have seen or talked to a doctor or other health care professional about their own health in the past 12 months, by sex and age group—National health interview survey, United States, 2015 | MMWR.* Center for Disease Control and Prevention. https: //www.cdc.gov/mmwr/volumes/66/wr/mm6602a12. htm

Vaillancourt, K. T. (2006). *Reconstructing the meaning of fidelity: A qualitative inquiry into swinging* relationships.* Virginia Polytechnic Institute and State University.

Valdes, F., Culp, J. M., & Harris, A. (2002). Battles wages, won, and lost: Critical race theory at the turn of the new millennium. In F. Valdes, J. M. Culp, & A. Harris (Eds.), Crossroads, directions and a new critical race theory. Philadelphia: Temple University Press.

Vock, D. C. (2021, June 13). *Teachers come under pressure as politicians, parents battle over 'critical race theory.* 'Kansas Reflector. https: //kansasreflector.com/2021/06/13/teachers-come-under-pressure-as-politicians-parents-battle-over-critical-race-theory/?eType=EmailBlastContent&eId=1c7c5654–9a2a-47bf-89b7–92e9b731eeb8

Vrentas, J., & Belson, K. (2022, March 29). *Brian Flores's Lawsuit Looms Over N. F. L. Owners Meetings.* The New York Times. https: //www.nytimes.com/2022/03/28/sports/football/brian-flores-lawsuit-nfl-owners.html

Wamser-Nanney, R. (2021). Understanding gun violence: Factors associated with beliefs regarding guns, gun policies, and gun violence. *Psychology of Violence, 11*(4), 349.

Waters, E., & Sroufe, L. A. (1983). Social competence as a developmental construct. *Developmental Review, 3*(1), 79–97.

Watson. F., (2013). *Facing the Black Shadow.* BookBaby.

Westcott, K. (2015). Race, criminalization, and historical trauma in the united states: Making the case for a new justice framework. *Traumatology: An International Journal, 21*(4), 273–84. doi: http: //dx.doi.org/10.1037/trm0000048

Wester, S. R. (2008). Male gender role conflict and multiculturalism: Implications for counseling psychology. *The Counseling Psychologist, 36*(2), 294–324. doi: http: //dx.doi.org.www2.1ib.ku.edu/10.1177/0011000006286341

White, J. L., & Cones, J. H. (1999). *Black man emerging: Facing the past and seizing a future in America.* New York: Freeman.

White, M. and Epston, D. (1990) *Narrative means to therapeutic ends.* W. W. Norton, New York.

World Health Organization. Lead poisoning and health. (2019, August 29). Retrieved April 24, 2021, from https: //www.who.int/newsroom/fact-sheets/detail/lead-poisoning-and-health

Wu, K. K., Chan, S. K., and Ma, T. M. (2005). Posttraumatic stress after SARS. *Emerging Infectious Diseases* 11, 1297–1300. doi: 10.3201/eid1108.041083

Xiao, Y., Becerik-Gerber, B., Lucas, G., & Roll, S. C. (2021). Impacts of working from home during COVID-19 pandemic on physical and mental well-being of office workstation users. *Journal of Occupational and Environmental Medicine, 63*(3), 181–90. https: //doi.org/10.1097/JOM.0000000000002097

Yang, D., Sheki, U., Tu, C., & Dai, X. (2020). Psychological effects of the COVID-19 pandemic on wuhan's high school students. *Children and Youth Services Review, 119*, 9. doi: http: //dx.doi.org/10.1016/j.childyouth.2020.105634

Yates, T. M., Egeland, B., & Sroufe, L. A. (2003). Rethinking resilience: A development process perspective.

Zacks, J. M. (2015). *Flicker: Your brain on movies*. Oxford: *Oxford University Press.*

Zonta, M. (2019, July). *Racial disparities in home appreciation implications of the racially segmented housing market for african-americans' equity building and the enforcement of fair housing policies.* Center for American Progress. https: //www.americanprogress.org/issues/economy/reports/2019/07/15/469838/racial-disparities-home-appreciation/

Made in the USA
Monee, IL
13 October 2023

44539198R00136